# Guide to
# Living in a
# Democracy

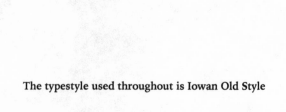

The typestyle used throughout is Iowan Old Style

*To the memory of my cousin Nita Schechet*
*who reminded us of the words of Abrahan Lincoln*
*as a guide for what is required for democracy to survive:*
*"We must disenthrall ourselves."*[1]

# Guide to Living in a Democracy

*by*

Steve Zolno

REGENT PRESS
Berkeley, California
2022

paperback:

ISBN 13: 978-1-58790-626-8

ISBN 10: 1-58790-626-0


e-book:

ISBN 13: 978-1-58790-627-5

ISBN: 10: 1-58790-627-9


Library of Congress Cataloging-in-Publication Data
(forthcoming)

Cover Photo: First Reading of the Emancipation Proclamation
by President Lincoln (1864), by Francis Bicknell Carpenter
(1830–1900).

Lincoln presented the Emancipation Proclamation to his
Cabinet on July 22, 1862, and issued the Proclamation on
September 22, 1862, which took effect on January 1, 1863.

Manufactured in the U.S.A.
Regent Press
Berkeley, California
www.regentpress.net
regentpress@mindspring.com

# Contents

# INTRODUCTION

This is the story of democracy.

It also is the story of the deep aspiration within every human being to be recognized as a valid and worthwhile individual. It is about how that aspiration has been honored – and dishonored – throughout time. It is about how human dignity is essential to the success of democracy. And it is about how simple acts – based on basic principles – can make the world work for all of us.

As first expressed in the US Constitution – and later echoed by numerous constitutions around the world – establishing government by and for "We the people" is the main aspiration of democracy.[2] It is to this principle we must continuously recommit ourselves if our democracies are to survive. This is how we move toward a world where we all are recognized for our value as members of society.

Looking after our individual needs is a basic human attribute. But at some point people realized that combining efforts toward the common good benefited them and improved their chances of survival. We each have a democratic impulse that recognizes the value of others and wants to collaborate toward what works best for all. We also have an autocratic impulse that prefers authority and is more comfortable leading or being led. In human history, the autocratic side has been prevalent.

Democracy has shown itself intermittently after we first sat together as families and small tribes and cooperated to meet our needs.[3] At the level of government, it raised its head in ancient Athens and Rome, and then again unsteadily after the 1215 Magna Carta in England, until beginning to bloom after the American Revolution.[4] It slowly has been blossoming since that time as the worth of individuals of all backgrounds and ethnicities has become more accepted. Yet autocracy – the rule of one leader or group – continues to be a threat to the freedom and fair treatment of everyone.

Our thoughts about others are affected by our experience and what we are told. We might consider some people worthy of our trust and others threatening. We may think we see people clearly, but have our vision clouded by ideas from our past or upbringing. If we are driven mainly by our beliefs, we will have a less accurate view of others and thus be less able to focus together on common goals.[5]

Our attitudes and actions move us closer to, or further from, a society that serves us all. That depends on whether the knowledge we glean from the past can be adapted to meet the needs of the present. Democracy remains viable when we open ourselves to updating our vision, as we have done in the US for over 200 years. When we cling to beliefs that no longer serve us, our actions become less effective at making our democracies work.

Real democracy protects the rights of everyone at all levels of society. It can be brought into our families, schools, institutions, and governments. Situations where the rights of some are ignored to accommodate those of others no longer are democratic. This includes anywhere that one group furthers its interests while disregarding the common good.

Democracies do not stand still. They slide backwards unless continually renewed, thus perpetual vigilance is required by those who support them. Maintaining our democracies requires ongoing dialogue based on a common vision of human equality, and then making changes based on that dialogue.[6]

Throughout history, the deterioration of

revolutions into autocracies provides a cautionary tale. In our day we see the faltering of democratic ideals throughout the world – from Europe, to Asia, to Africa, to Central and South America, and even in the United States. Much of this is the result of a failure to genuinely commit ourselves to principles and actions based on upholding human dignity. When we treat others with less than total dignity, we move toward a world where the rights of everyone will be threatened, including our own.

Many politicians and political parties make promises to promote democratic principles, but upon taking office focus primarily on maintaining their own power. In some countries – such as Russia and China – meaningful elections have been eliminated. In democracies such as the US, failure by leaders to acknowledge the value of every individual – and act on that principle – has resulted in discontent by those who believe their needs are ignored. This can result in people losing faith in democracy and blindly following those who claim to have the answers.[7]

There are numerous tales in our myths and religions about how we once were inhabitants of a nearly perfect world, how we lost that world, and in the process nearly destroyed ourselves. The story of the Garden of Eden in the Bible is one.[8] We carry a vision of that perfect world in our minds and blame others – or the circumstances of our lives – for falling short. We may think those who stand in our way should be criticized or even eliminated. This has been the source of much strife throughout history.

We need a vision to guide our actions. We rely on a mental image of the world to plan where we are going and what we will do. Our interactions with others are guided by how we view them. Seeing all people as equally valid individuals moves us in the direction of democracy. A view that some are more worthy than others is the essence of autocracy. Our worst crises and deprivations have been the result of seeing people as "the other," or the enemy, rather than acknowledging our common humanity. The result has been a series of calamities – including wars and mass starvation – that exceed any punishment that nature can impose.

The natural world presents challenges via fires, storms, earthquakes and other disasters, but our greatest threat is our own actions toward each other. There is nothing from which our civilization cannot recover if we dedicate ourselves to the idea that every human being has value. In democracies we often respond to disasters with generosity on a massive scale. As we care for others we experience being cared about and are more likely to be helped when our time of need comes. Those of an autocratic mindset tend to be isolated, which decreases the likelihood they will be moved to help those in need.

We all hope for solutions to the crises of our time. The reality of our world is complex, but often we are guided by limited and inflexible views that blind us to the bigger picture of our common needs. It is the responsibility of those who believe in democracy to keep an open mind rather than being swayed by a partisan perspective. We need to commit ourselves to putting our judgments of others aside if we expect that we also will be treated fairly. When we move toward a vision of a functioning and compassionate society we start to solve our dilemmas. Some will fail to commit to a democratic vision, but waiting for them only will delay moving forward.

For democracy to thrive, what applies to one must apply to all. This is the essence of fairness, and should be embodied not only in our laws, but in our everyday actions. Democracy must be taught in our schools and expressed in conversations by those who value it. Its spirit must be inscribed on our hearts as well as in our minds. We move toward that world by combining efforts toward common understanding and action. But when we focus on blaming others we mainly hurt ourselves.

Democracy is most vulnerable when we assume it is forever safe. There never has been, nor will there ever be, such a time. To guarantee its preservation, we must continually remind ourselves about what it is, what it looks like in the real world, and how to bring it into play.

Constitutions are no guarantee of democracy. All constitutions promise democratic government,[9] but in many countries those are empty words that mask tyranny. In our day we see a shrinking of democratic principles around the world. This began in Russia after the fall of the Soviet Union, and now has affected countries on every inhabited continent. In the last twenty years, democracy has diminished in too many places to list: Hungary, Poland, Venezuela, the Philippines, Zimbabwe, and Egypt among them.

A recent attempt to overthrow democracy in the US is a wound that still festers, and threatens to reopen. Nations – or factions within nations – justify violence against others by violating values and institutions based on human equality. They defend their actions by blaming their victims. This happened in the American South during the persecution of Blacks for over 100 years after the Civil War, and was used by Nazi propagandists in their persecution of the Jews. It is being seen in the war by Russia against Ukraine. But not since the Civil War have we witnessed in the United States the defense of a violent insurrection by most members of a major political party.

The confrontation between autocracy and democracy continues, and perhaps always will. We must choose whether to join the forces that support human rights, or lead our lives in the hope that the threat will go away. But just hoping that autocracy never arrives at our door may pave a path for losing our democracy.

This book is not about condemning people, which only sets up a contest about who is right or wrong. It is about the essential element of respect that must be brought into democratic situations, from the interpersonal to the international, if they are to guarantee human rights. This means we must commit ourselves to upholding the dignity of every human being – both personally and politically – to maintain our own.

Those who choose autocracy are not bad

people – they just fail to see the larger picture of what works best for everyone, themselves included. It is up to the rest of us to help them see that.

When stuck in a mode of blame we are unable to move forward toward a world that works for all. We only progress toward a democratic vision by focusing in concert with others, then following through on a plan of action. When the US framers wrote the Declaration of Independence, they listed their grievances, but mainly emphasized their "right to be independent states." Martin Luther King focused mainly on human dignity;[10] Gandhi warned his followers of the harm that hatred would have on them;[11] Nelson Mandela, despite 27 years in prison, wrote and spoke of a free society for people of all races.[12]

This book is about what the democratic vision looks like and how to make it a lived reality in our lives and nations. By our actions – or inactions – we will determine whether it is sustained for our own generation and those of the future. Actions that bring us together in a common cause – based on human dignity – lead us closer to a democracy that serves everyone, but focusing primarily on who or what we are against threatens its very existence.

I want to acknowledge the support I received in editing and improving this book from Barry Eichengreen, Curtis Estes, David Shiner, Dennis Kaplan, Ethel Murphy, Judith Linzer, Rob Katz and Sharon Chelton. With their suggestions I hopefully have been able to shine a light on the most essential actions required for those who hope to maintain their democracies now and in the future. The views expressed herein – and the book's shortcomings – are the responsibility of the author.

# A BRIEF HISTORY
# OF DEMOCRACY

No one knows when what we would now call democracy began.

Cooperation is an essential element of survival. Those who study the behavior of animals and tribal humans tell us that cooperation is seen in both.[13] Competition – between individuals and groups – is important for motivation, but cooperation is needed to build societies and governments that last.[14] Success depends on a shared vision, as well as agreement on a plan for how to work toward – and achieve – that vision.

Before the dawn of civilization, our ancestors needed to act together to bring down their prey. They shared a common vision of how they would proceed on the hunt. Did they join forces because a leader guided their every move, or did they collaborate in advance on a plan to ensure success? We can be fairly certain that the hunt was more successful when there was a plan that everyone understood and in which all cooperated.

According to many anthropologists, there was a great amount of shared decision making in primitive societies. With the gradual advent of language over at least 50,000 years, humans were able to work together and succeed far beyond the level of their non-verbal ancestors.[15] This led them to eventually inhabit the globe.

Tribes grew into states and then nations. As they became larger, greater authority was concentrated in fewer hands. People began to accept divisions between those at the top and bottom. In ancient Egypt, rulers were considered gods, and in China the emperor was called the Son of Heaven. But people always have valued their freedom. They rebelled against what they considered tyranny everywhere because they saw themselves as more than just animals expected to do what they were told; they considered themselves individuals deserving of respect and dignity.

The democratic impulse to make decisions by consensus has waxed and waned in human society as far back as we can see. The advent of democracy in government promised to uphold human rights while maintaining the protections of living in a society.

## *Ancient Greece*

Early Greece was composed of city-states run by rulers, like most civilizations of the time. In 594 BCE, Solon, who codified Athenian law, saw the negative effect on society as peasants became increasingly indebted to their creditors and fell into servitude. He took the unprecedented step of eliminating debt bondage and allowed representatives from different economic classes to participate in government.[16]

About 100 years later, Athens thrived under what many historians consider the first democratic government. Citizens drew lots to determine who would serve in the legislative body – or Assembly – and on juries. This was a radical departure from the past and other contemporary cultures. Citizens discussed their roles and responsibilities to the state as they helped shape the norms by which they would be governed.[17] Yet only about 10% of the population of 300,000 was allowed to participate. Women, slaves, children and those who were not citizens were excluded.

The Athenians were proud of their democracy. According to Pericles, the great statesman who built the Acropolis, the religious and civic center on a hill overlooking the city:

*Our constitution does not copy the laws of neighboring states; we are rather a pattern to others than imitators ourselves. Its administration favors the many instead of the few; this is why it is called a democracy. If we look to the laws, they afford equal justice to all in their private differences; if no social standing, advancement in public life falls to reputation for capacity, class considerations not being allowed to interfere with merit; nor again does poverty bar the way, if a man is able to serve the state, he is not hindered by the obscurity of his condition.[18]*

Athens also had brushes with oligarchy, and imposed cruel domination on city-states that were forced to be part of their military coalition. Like many societies before and since, those who ruled Athens, despite its democracy, did not welcome questioning of their lifestyle and institutions. They voted to execute Socrates – a popular philosopher – in 399 BCE for "corrupting the youth," that is, teaching them to question authority. Athens went into slow decline after its defeat by Sparta in 404 BCE.

## *Rome*

Rome became a republic as the result of a revolution in 509 BCE, after which it was ruled by its citizens, represented by consuls elected for one year. That eventually gave way to the Senate, which engaged in dialogue to formulate laws.[19] Often there was ongoing tension between ordinary citizens (plebeians) and the wealthy (patricians). The Senate eventually had 600 members who served for life and elected their own replacements, which deepened the rift between rulers and those who were ruled.

In 63 BCE a plot to overturn the Republic was foiled. Then there was an attempt at tyranny when a triumvirate – Pompey, Julius Caesar, and Marcus Crassus – decided to "fix the political system in their own interests."[20] Rome went from being a republic to an autocracy under Augustus Caesar in 27 BCE, and extended its reach to the entire known world over the next two hundred years. Citizenship was available to those in conquered lands if they submitted to Roman law. The Roman Empire collapsed around 400 AD as it became overextended and vulnerable to incursion. Western society regressed, with leadership reverting to local authorities. The situation was similar in Asia and the Middle East.

## *The Middle Ages*

As the Roman Empire fell, much of Europe was divided into fiefdoms under local kings with serfs working the land. In Western Europe there was an element of democracy: serfs often were able to negotiate the terms of their contracts due to labor shortages brought on by high mortality from plague and a large percent of children failing to survive.[21]

The Holy Roman Empire, founded under Charlemagne, who was crowned by Pope Leo III in 800, conquered and governed central Europe in the name of the Church. Universities were developed for instruction in religion, but scientific and philosophic inquiry into the truths of the universe slowly gained ground. Some church leaders tied religious faith to rational enquiry, as did Thomas Aquinas in his *Summa Theologica*.

Science slowly superseded church doctrine. In the area of health, evidence showed hygiene to be more effective than prayer at saving lives. Exploration confirmed that ships could get to the East by sailing west.

## *The Renaissance*

The Renaissance followed the Middle Ages in Western Europe starting about 1400, but there always was a gradual evolution from one period to another. Human life became more valued for itself rather than mainly as a vehicle to the afterlife, a movement that was called "humanism." The Church was forced to share power with leaders throughout Europe. Regional authority slowly merged into nations. Much of Eastern Europe, as well as most of Asia, remained in a feudal state at this time.

The Renaissance flowed from a renewed interest in the dignity of the individual.[22]Although there remained a financial divide between the wealthiest members of society and the rest, the importance of education and art for those at all levels was beginning to be recognized. Books were more readily available due to the invention of the printing press. Knowledge contained in books, once considered the realm of only a few, was spread to more of the population via libraries. Some people were able to read the Bible for themselves and questioned the authority of the Church. This led to the advent of Protestant sects that eventually flourished.

As more people moved into towns, they began to specialize and develop trades, which increased general prosperity. Weekly markets became common. Money, in the form of coins issued by local governments, facilitated trade. Taxes were collected and used for the common good, to build roads and bridges for example.

## The Industrial Revolution

Starting in the 1700s, manufacturers began to mass produce goods cheaply and efficiently. Items such as clothing were made in factories that forced workers – often women and children – to labor in crowded and dangerous conditions for long hours and poor pay. Cities like Paris, Manchester, London, New York, Philadelphia and Boston expanded to accommodate the influx of workers. Mining of coal and iron expanded to fuel the factories, as did the need to transport large quantities of cotton and wool. In the US, mills were operated mainly by water power. Venture capital poured in to fuel the transition.[23] In the American South, the economy remained based primarily on cotton and tobacco.

A new class of oligarchs emerged who held monopolies in areas such as shipping and mining. They placed a stranglehold on

competition, and used their influence to prevent laws from restricting their monopolies.
The largest of them collaborated on agreements as how best to divide their industries, which eventually became trusts yield-
ing tremendous power. In the US the inter-
state Commerce Act (1887) eventually led to
these monopolies being broken up. President
Theodore Roosevelt complained about "A riot
of individualistic materialism."[24]

Factory workers formed unions to demand
better pay and working conditions, but
these struggles often were accompanied by
strikes that resulted in attacks on workers by
agents of employers or governments, sometimes resulting in serious injury or death.[25]
Eventually unions were able to negotiate a
reduction in child labor and working hours as
well as an increase in wages. Some employers,
such as Henry Ford in the early 1900s, saw the
benefit of paying higher wages to employees
that allowed them to make purchases which
improved their lives as well as the economy.

## Modern Democracies

The evolution of democratic ideas in
Western Europe was very gradual. In 1215,
members of the aristocracy in England forced

King John, an unpopular monarch, to sign what became known as the Magna Carta. It provided them protection from arbitrary arrest and required their consent to levy taxes. Although originally applying only to the relationship between the king and his barons, the significance of the Magna Carta on English law was debated for hundreds of years. It eventually led to English Common Law that, at least in theory, applied equally to those at all levels of society.

The movement toward democracy was spurred beginning around the year 1700 by the writings of those known as the Enlightenment authors, including John Locke[26] in England, Jean Jacques Rousseau[27] and Charles Montesquieu[28] in France. Thomas Paine provided direct inspiration for the American Revolution in his pamphlet *Common Sense,* and Patrick Henry in his 1775 fiery speech that began: "Give me liberty or give me death." In the next century, John Stuart Mill greatly influenced thinking about democracy in his book *On Liberty*: "The practical question, [is] where to place the limit – how to make the fitting adjustment between individual independence and social control."[29] This is a question we will consider at length in these pages.

## *The US Declaration of Independence*

In 1776, the US founders wrote their Declaration of Independence to declare themselves free from the domination of the King of England. The main author of the Declaration was Thomas Jefferson,[30] who wrote and rewrote it repeatedly after weeks of consultation with his co–authors, who included Benjamin Franklin and John Adams. Its most famous passage states:

*We hold these Truths to be self-evident, that all Men are created equal, that they are endowed by their Creator with certain unalienable Rights, that among these are Life, Liberty and the pursuit of happiness. That to secure these Rights, Governments are instituted among Men, deriving their just Powers from the Consent of the Governed, that whenever any Form of Government becomes destructive of these ends, it is the Right of the People to alter or to abolish it, and to institute new Government, laying its Foundation on such Principles, and organizing its Powers in such Form, as to them shall seem most likely to affect their Safety and happiness.*

If we were to agree on the direction that democracy should take, it would be based on the view expressed in this statement, updated for our day to include women. It provides the founding principles needed to guide us in preserving our democracies. The meaning and application of these words have been debated since the Declaration was adopted. It is not law but a statement of principles upon which the country was founded.

During the creation of the US, there were vast disagreements about what form the new government should take. The founders wanted to free themselves from what they considered the tyranny of the English King, but the direction of the new country was at first unclear. Some wanted George Washington as King. The Declaration of Independence stated that the guiding principle would be equal rights, but the country floundered under the Articles of Confederation that failed to provide a strong central authority.

Since the establishment of the United States, more than 100 nations have come into existence that claim to be democracies, but as we will see, many more nations promise these privileges to their citizens than actually grant them.

## *The US Constitution*

Since the founders understood they would not have a viable nation unless they came together under a common vision, unity eventually prevailed. The US Constitution, written in 1787 after four intense months of negotiation, specified a path forward. It completed the second – and most important – part of the revolution. This is the exception in history. It is relatively easy for people to unite in common effort against tyranny or a threat, but much more challenging to create and move toward a model of what they want to put in its place. Many revolutions end in failure because they are unable to take this essential step.

The United States was the first government to establish a written Constitution that applied to all its citizens. That Constitution, which is the highest law of the land, begins with this Preamble:

*We the people of the United States, in order to form a more perfect union, establish justice, insure domestic tranquility, provide for the common defense, promote the general welfare, and secure the blessings of liberty to ourselves and our posterity, do ordain and establish this Constitution for the United States of America.*

The Preamble is not considered by courts to be binding law itself, but provides guidance for how the rest of the US Constitution is to be interpreted. Those who wrote it created a document that reflected the most progressive thinking of their time. Ever since, democracies around the world have been challenged by conflict between the interests of the individual or group, and those of society as a whole.

In the early days of the young country, Americans were appreciative of the freedoms they had gained, although many, including women, slaves, Native Americans and those who did not own property, were denied those freedoms, including the right to vote. It was nevertheless a radical experiment for its time. Legislators, as well as ordinary people, disagreed on major issues like slavery and who should be able to vote, but the country was held together by a common dedication to the vision prescribed by the Constitution. Civic engagement was widespread among the many who read newspapers and attended political rallies.[31]

As often happens after revolutions, unity faded.[32] Americans began to take their freedoms for granted. Rather than focusing on resolving issues, they began to lay blame on each other. Compromises on slavery, for example, that had been worked out during the writing of the Constitution, gave way to an unwillingness to address that issue based on the founding principle of human equality. The Civil War was the result. It cost over 700,000 lives among soldiers and civilians of all races and destroyed the economy of the South. Then, and now, in the words of Lincoln: "A house divided cannot stand."[33]

Since that time, much of the discourse in the US has continued to be about who to blame for the nation's ills rather than how to resolve issues for mutual benefit. Most of the country was able to come together at times of war, when the external enemy was clear, especially during and after the Second World War, when democracy itself was under threat. After the spirit of unity brought on by that war, and the economic boom that followed, divisions again emerged and often have dominated the national dialogue.

Divisiveness harms those on both sides of the divide. As people spend their energy focusing on who and what they are against, they are less likely to work together for mutual benefit. They often follow their chosen leader or political party while ignoring their common cause that brings movement toward resolution. Legislation stalls while politicians engage in conflict. Infrastructure – including roads and bridges – deteriorates while economic inequality becomes entrenched.[34]

As happened in Greece and Rome, our tendency to blame others – rather than engage in dialogue toward common solutions – keeps us from implementing the democratic vision that we all are equally valuable human beings. The functioning of our lives and countries becomes diminished.

Politicians often advance their careers by telling followers who or what to be against. This does nothing to meet the real needs of their followers. To move us forward, leaders must clarify what they are for rather than what they are against, and how it will be achieved. We need to demand that they share their vision of a world that includes meeting the needs of everyone, and specifically how they are going to implement that vision. Some tell us there are many truths and thus all views are equally valid. This is a false equivalency; hate and blame never are equal to respectful human interaction. When we say: "I hate," we are hurting ourselves whether or not it affects the object of our hatred.

In countries where democracy is threatened, many have surrendered their right to think independently. They have given over the major decisions that affect them to their leaders. They believe that dialogue no longer is needed. Leaders who promise to "fix it all" never focus on the needs of their country because their emphasis is on keeping themselves in power. They fail to fulfill the democratic vision as they prioritize their interests and those of their supporters.[35] Followers who don't recognize that their leaders have shortcomings have adopted an autocratic mindset. As the American founders and those who inspired them advocated, entrenched and uncompromising autocracy justifies its removal.

To maintain human rights in one country, it is necessary to support them in others. Democratic governments can fall in country after country as an autocratic mindset spreads. Rebellions also can spread, as did the American Revolution that inspired that of France and many others around the world. But in the twentieth century, Russia[36] and China[37] are the leading examples of failed revolutions. Countries once under the Soviet Bloc, such as Poland and Hungary,[38] as well as many in the Middle and Far East, South and Central America, are losing their democratic thrust to autocratic leaders and one-party rule.

Because of a failure to implement the crucial second step of clarifying the type of government that is to replace autocracy, revolutions in many countries have lost the democracies they sought to establish. Those who support autocratic leaders don't understand that when freedoms are denied to some, they soon will be denied to everyone. The way to continue moving toward our democratic goals is to use dialogue to establish a common understanding of what best serves the needs of everyone.

Even within the US, the country many consider the most successful democracy in history, there remains a conflict between stated ideals and how they are to be applied in the real world. Many of its founders held slaves even while expressing the ideal of human equality in its founding documents. Slavery was officially declared illegal when Lincoln issued the Emancipation Proclamation during the Civil War, but the rights of Blacks and other minorities to vote and to equal justice often still are denied.[39] [40] [41]

Constitutions never are adequate to ensure human rights. Implementation of the freedoms promised by democracy is a never-ending process to which we must commit ourselves to maintain them. We cannot simply leave our fate in the hands of leaders, assuming all will be well. Maintaining our freedoms requires advocating for them in our personal and political lives to ensure that they – and those of others – benefit future generations as well as our own.

# THE CHALLENGE OF DEMOCRACY

The struggle between autocratic and democratic elements always has been with us.

Those who started the American Revolution were the radicals of their day. They believed that they and their freedoms mattered in the face of what they considered British oppression, and were willing to risk everything to overthrow it. But when they wrote the Constitution, they considered White males to be "the people."[42]

Since that time – after many hard-fought struggles – more have been included in what is meant by "We the people." Blacks, women, persons with disabilities, those in same-sex relationships, and many others now are considered valid human beings who are equal under the law, at least in theory. We slowly are coming to understand that government by and for only some of the people is not really democracy. Maintaining a system of laws or customs that recognize the rights of everyone is a challenge. Every nation that considers itself democratic falls short.

Even in the earliest societies, aggression needed to be curbed. Rules and laws – at first verbal and then written – were created by societies that had grown too large to resolve issues by personal interaction. The laws of Mesopotamia, for example, which preceded the Bible, prescribed punishments for those who harmed others, which is the origin of the term "an eye for an eye."[43]

Because of our long story going back into prehistory, we each have conflicting impulses. We have gone to the moon and beyond, but still often are ruled by primitive emotions. Attitudes and actions based on both personal and group needs have become part of our nature. We want to develop and use our individual skills, but also want to comply with what our leaders tell us to believe and do. We want to make the major decisions that affect us, but also want to align with the traditions of our cultures. We want to run our own lives, but give authority to those we trust to lead us in the right direction.[44]

We hope that giving responsibility to leaders frees us to go about our daily activities; that rules and laws will guard us against aggression; that we will be treated fairly in disputes; that our government will provide internal order and protect us from external forces.[45]

When people believe that their leaders fail them, they may protest or revolt. They might overthrow a government they see as oppressive in hope that a new system will provide greater freedom and opportunity. But rebellions often give way to greater oppression. Many revolutions overthrow autocratic regimes only to result in worse autocracy.

There is a long list of nations where leaders of rebellions have tried to establish greater human rights, and also a long list of places where they have failed. The desire of those in countries once under control of the Soviet Union to move in the direction of democracy – Poland, Hungary, and Belarus among them – has largely been crushed.[46] But feeling the threat to their own sovereignty after the invasion of Ukraine by Russia, Poland and Hungary are suddenly becoming aware of the need to work with other Western democracies.

The 2011 "Arab Spring" in the Middle East has been suppressed in every country where it once gave hope, including Egypt, Syria, and Libya. Other countries that once had a semblance of democracy – the Philippines, Burma, and Nicaragua to name a few – now are turning toward greater autocracy. Even in long-established democracies, there are large "populist" movements working to create division by claiming they are oppressed and that minorities are ruining their country: the United States, United Kingdom, France and Germany among them.

Nowhere is democracy totally safe. There are some countries where it remains largely successful, among them Canada, the Scandinavian nations, and notably Estonia. But even these have "populist" movements that champion the rights of some over others.[47]

So overthrowing oppression does not necessarily lead to greater freedom. It doesn't guarantee that people will be able to make the major decisions that affect their lives – including freedom of movement, choosing a vocation, how or if to worship, and other daily choices that those in democracies take for granted. Rebellion doesn't necessarily lead to an improved system of government that will bring freedom of the press, create economic security, guarantee free speech, let people vote for their leaders, or allow them to pursue their dreams.

We might ask ourselves two essential questions: (1) How has democracy become diminished in so many places in our day? and (2)

How do we restore the momentum toward genuine democracy around the world? Answering these questions, and acting on what we learn, will guide us toward safeguarding the rights of everyone, including our own.

Where democracies are successful at protecting human rights and choices, most people forget the long struggle of uniting against oppression that brought them their independence. They settle into daily routines and fail to monitor their leaders. They may allow their countries to turn back in the direction of oppression by supporting politicians who champion the rights of some over others. Autocracy can creep up gradually so that people barely notice until they have allowed the establishment of an oppressive regime that serves itself in their name and is a threat to the freedom of everyone.[48] Many leaders throughout history have attempted to install themselves permanently after having been elected to office.

Complacency is the greatest danger to democracy. Only continual vigilance and advocacy can preserve it. If the rights of any of us are diminished, the rights of all are threatened. If we wish to maintain democracy for ourselves we need to champion it for everyone, even those with whom we disagree. Thus the freedoms of all are intertwined. We harm democracy, and ourselves, by ignoring the humanity of others. As we regress into autocracy, we establish by our attitudes, words and actions that some people matter more than others. If we believe in democracy, we insist that no human being is superior to any other. We support others in maintaining their rights as we would want them to support us.

Our success as humans is largely based on an ability to adapt to new and changing conditions. We have gained skills unmatched by any species, which has allowed us to expand across the planet. Our lives – and civilizations – are shaped by decisions based on our limited perceptions of the world, others and ourselves. Our continued success depends on appreciating our strengths and limits as we build greater understanding, which is a lifelong process. Humility always is in order because our concepts fall short of reality. This is why dialogue is needed at both the personal and political level to expand our understanding of how we best can maintain our democracies in concert with others.

Those who wrote the US Constitution were more than rebels; they were visionaries who described, in broad strokes, but considerable detail, how a democratic republic might function. They left room for reform over time. They understood human nature, perhaps imperfectly, but saw that we combine a rational side that considers our long-term interests and sets expectations for how we should act, with an irrational and selfish side that ignores the larger picture.[49] The founders themselves often embodied that contradiction by engaging in personal attacks on each other when not joining together for their common cause.[50]

We all are flawed individuals. We can be consumed by judgment or recognize that imperfection is part of our nature. We can continually be in conflict due to the shortcomings we see in others, or we can cooperate despite our imperfections. As we recognize each other as valid beings, we acknowledge our common humanity and are able to move forward.

Holding on to any view too rigidly can blind us to reality and make our actions less effective. In our daily lives, as in the hunt long ago, inflexible ideas can cause us to miss the mark. We can move past rigidity by acknowledging our limits and opening to the possibility that the world may differ from the way we see it. Paying greater attention – and opening to the views of others guided by respect for human integrity, as well as current scientific insights – allows us to interact more effectively with a world that is continually changing. It enables us to function as best we can in tune with the truth of what is around us and the view most compatible with survival.

In democracies, "We the people" participate in the best system yet devised to advance the human race by seeing that we all have common needs – both physical and emotional – and supporting each other in meeting those needs. We can continue moving toward that vision while realizing that our quest may never be complete.

Knowing we don't want autocracy is different from maintaining democracy. History, in our discussions and curriculums, can be our guide to help clarify the actions needed to keep democracy viable for ourselves and future generations. Our mistakes, as well as successes, must be confronted if we are to move forward.

Our judgments divide us and our compassion unites us. If our everyday conversations – and our educational systems – focus on discussing and understanding the type of government that best recognizes the value of every human being, we will move toward implementing that vision. It's easy to dwell on shortcomings, but clarifying a path of action is how we become part of the solution to what ails us.

Democracy is threatened throughout the world and in every country that considers itself democratic. Its light is barely discernible in places where it once burned brightly. If we don't protect it everywhere, those threats will inevitably arrive at our door, introduced from without and within. But the solution is in our hands. With real populism that values not just our own group, but everyone and their rights, we can turn the tide back toward democracy.

Below I describe some of the essential guiding principles of democracy, how we have failed, and how we can succeed. We each must choose whether we are on the side of human equality, or of partisan interests that undermine the foundations of a free society.

The most essential question to ask ourselves and others is: "Are you on the side of democracy? And if so, are you going to take the necessary steps to move us toward a country and world that works for everyone, not just a few?"

Our answer – and our actions based on it – will determine whether democracy will be preserved.

# GUIDING PRINCIPLES
# OF DEMOCRACY

# First Guiding Principle of Democracy

*Constructive Dialogue*

Democracy is forged in dialogue.

From the time of our earliest origins, our behavior has been shaped by understanding that what benefits the group also benefits the individual. We are social beings not only because we enjoy interaction with others, but because social behavior improves our chances of survival. It is what makes us fully human.

Every successful democracy has been built on conversations between people about how they can meet their common needs. Cooperation to create and work toward a vision of how to sustain our democracies is what makes them viable. The unique part of the American Revolution was not that it began in rebellion, but that the founders prescribed a viable path forward.

The principle of "government by the

people" is far from being fully implemented by any country in our day. If we want to keep our democracies, we must continually engage in constructive dialogue about how we can maintain them. This applies to our legislators and each of us in our personal conversations. If we focus only on meeting the needs of some, we are moving in the direction of autocracy, which ultimately must fail because it disregards the needs of many who eventually rise in revolt. But what replaces autocracy is not always democratic.

Competition and cooperation both are parts of human nature. Within each of us lies an impulse to advance ourselves at the expense of others. We often would rather emphasize the shortcomings of another than cooperate to create a society that serves us all. We may think we're acting in our best interests when we engage in blame or destructive dialogue. But these behaviors harm us – and those around us – by making our governments and lives less stable. They result in a breakdown of the cooperative spirit that makes democracy work. Although competition appeals to our need for recognition, cooperation is what moves us forward. Extreme competition that leads to advancing some, while leaving others behind, moves democracy backward.

Democracies tend to be in flux. Ancient Athens and Rome became democratic for a while, but reverted back to autocracy before their ultimate demise. In the twentieth century, Russia and China overthrew autocracies then installed even more oppressive regimes. Russia briefly became a democracy after the 1991 collapse of the Soviet Union, but that now has been lost, although large protests still erupt at times. After its 1949 revolution, Communist China, which calls itself "The People's Republic of China," never fulfilled Marx's promise of a "dictatorship of the proletariat." Instead it simply has become a dictatorship. Many in that country also protest at their peril.[51]

In Western Europe, democracies are threatened by a "populist" wave that backs parties and leaders who emphasize the welfare of some while vilifying others. The US recently has experienced a similar attack on democracy by people who follow an autocratic leader who denigrates people. Many political observers think it uncertain if the US will be able to maintain its democracy.[52]

When we think our leader or party can do no wrong, we have fallen into the trap of autocracy. Once autocracies become entrenched, people often realize – too late – that they have given up their freedoms.[53] Autocratic leaders engage in any deception necessary to strengthen their following and stay in power that includes weakening the courts and outlawing opposition leaders.[54] Followers fail to understand that the real message they support is hatred and division, which are likely to be turned back on them.

Once in power, autocrats continually seek new scapegoats for what they claim are the problems of their country. They focus on real and imagined enemies – within their countries and without – to keep people distracted.[55] As their freedoms disappear, everyone comes under the thumb of oppression. Numerous examples from the past and present include regimes from the right and left. In the twentieth century – Communist China, Nazi Germany, Italy and the Soviet Union serve as examples – millions placed their trust in leaders who failed to provide the perfect society they promised. They then turned their countries into dictatorships while persecuting anyone who protested. The same has happened after numerous revolutions throughout history, from France in the late 1700s to the Middle East in our own time.

All constitutions promise democracy, even those of countries that are autocratic.[56]

The actual degree of freedom depends on whether there is a shared democratic vision.[57] In once-democratic countries that have turned authoritarian, government no longer is by "the people" or "consent of the governed." Voting, when allowed, is limited to pre-chosen candidates; freedom of speech and the press are outlawed; education serves government propaganda;[58] alternative views are suppressed; wealth is distributed to those who support the regime. Poverty becomes entrenched for many.

In a real democratic setting, problems that have the potential to affect everyone become shared. This increases the chance they will be addressed, whether it be employment loss, crop failure, natural disasters, or confronting inequality. This also is the basis of morality – we value each other not only because of esteem for one another, but because working together enhances our chances of success.

Labeling ourselves as "conservative" or "liberal" means little because views of leaders and political parties fluctuate. Many who consider themselves conservative have no well-thought out views; they hold to a vision of an imagined perfect time that never existed. Real conservatism is aligning with the value of universal respect upon which democracy is founded. Many who consider themselves liberals assume that conservatives have inferior views, which broadens the divide. Real liberalism is openness to considering the variety of forms that democracies can take.

Everyone wants some type of government. Even extreme individualists need a stable situation to protect their independence. Democratic government, when it works, involves cooperation on a large scale. We look to our elected representatives to manage our interests as equitably as possible. We delegate authority because we can't make consensual decisions about daily government functions, such as enforcing our laws or repairing our streets.

Our inveterate tribalism can lead us to believe that those we think of as different from us are not quite human, which justifies marginalizing or eliminating them. We choose whether to live in a world of hate and retribution, or one of mutual respect. Some believe that stability comes from elimination of those who stand in their way, but there always will be someone in the way.

What moves us forward – in our own lives and in democratic governments – is combining efforts toward our vision of a society that best serves us all. Once we agree, we must clarify the steps needed to progress toward that vision, and then commit to specific, verifiable ways by which we will follow through. Otherwise our agreements are unlikely to come to fruition.

People and their needs are more complex than the labels or concepts by which we view them. Every human being is different. The only way to clarify – and then move – toward solutions is to strive to achieve a common understanding of what best serves everyone. Trust – based on a common vision – allows easy transition from one step to the next as we pursue our goals. When we establish trust, every move no longer needs to be negotiated.

Patriotism is not blind devotion to a leader or country. Real patriotism in democracy is adherence to the principle of human equality. The best way to resolve what ails us is to admit that we fall short. This allows us to move toward solutions to the many areas before us that need attention, including our decaying infrastructure, the pollution that is choking us, climate change, educating our children to participate in democracy, a vibrant economy, and encouraging human rights at home and abroad. There will be much upon which we disagree, but a commitment to hearing each other and resolving issues is what makes democracy possible.

## *Where we went wrong*

Numerous revolutions have overthrown oppression in the hope of creating a more democratic government, but many have moved back in the direction of autocracy. They sacrificed their hard-won freedom by focusing on blame and prioritizing the needs of some over others. This has been the cause of the failure of many democracies in the past and in our own time.

## *How we get back on track*

Democracies only can be preserved by engaging in ongoing constructive dialogue among all players – including legislators and ordinary people – emphasizing how to "ensure the general welfare," as mentioned in the US Constitution. This allows them to be more productive and for us to be more fulfilled in our everyday lives.

# Second Guiding Principle of Democracy

## *Universal Respect*

The core of democracy is the principle of respect for every human being.

When we are born we feel connected to all we see around us, especially other people. What makes the company of young children enjoyable is their ability to universally accept others. This is the state of mind we left behind and to which we long to return.

The history of democracy is the story of how people have struggled to bring the ideals of human equality and dignity into everyday life. We have sought to balance individual rights with our responsibilities to society. Perhaps the oldest question reflected in our myths and stories is when and how to subordinate our interests to those of others – our leaders, our group, and our countries.

When states, and then nations, were ruled

by kings, queens or autocrats, the few who were favored by their leaders were considered the elite. When leaders catered mainly to their group of followers, many people resented that their needs were neglected, which often led to rebellion. But even successful rebellions usually resulted in replacing one ruler with another. The 1689 English Bill of Rights had the intent of making Parliament sovereign, but that did not take effect in a meaningful way for two hundred more years.

The exception was the American Revolution, which resulted in the first republic that recognized "We the people" as the source of power. The US founders were well-versed in history, yet they varied in their views about whether people could be trusted to govern themselves.[59] The government they created was innovative and unique for its time, based largely on the writings of "Enlightenment" authors who emphasized the dignity of every human being.[60] Over time we have come to better implement the vision of the founders, which they often failed to fulfill themselves.

Their statement that "All men are created equal," made it clear that their intent was the principle of universal respect, although the government they created was a limited expression of that ideal. Since then, our understanding of what that phrase means has greatly expanded.

Democracy, at its core, is the recognition of the validity of every human being. Despite how far we may be from fully implementing that principle, it remains our vision of how we might live in peace with others and ultimately within ourselves.

The founding documents of the United States are seen as models for democracies everywhere. People from countries where human rights are threatened or violated create an ever-expanding stream of refugees seeking the dignity and freedom they believe is their due, and hope will be theirs in the democracies where they aspire to live.

In the US, Britain, and other countries that believe themselves democratic, many people consider refugees a burden to be tolerated at best, and often held in disdain. The background of us all is that our forebears, or perhaps we ourselves, came from some other land seeking a better life, even those considered natives. If we want to live in a world where we and our aspirations are respected, we need to advocate that be the case for everyone. Those who came before us passed our freedoms on to us as a gift.

Respect from leaders in democracies is

shown by how we are addressed, by providing equal economic opportunities, by upholding our right to express our views, and by ensuring our ability to make the major decisions that affect our lives. Autocratic governments impose the interests of a limited group on the people as a whole.

If we believe in democracy, we support the rights and dignity of everyone, regardless of their background, level of ability, or group affiliation. We may be tempted to think that our views are superior, our finances better, or our children smarter than others, but we understand that nothing makes us more worthy than anyone else. When we put aside our assumptions about others, we see that no person, or group, is better than any other.

We each have unique talents and abilities. Our group identity – race, religion, gender, politics – only is a part, but not nearly the totality, of who we are. When we look past these outer trappings, we see more accurately into the essence of people. When we embrace diversity, rather than fearing it, we come to a deeper appreciation of others and ourselves. If our view of the world is constantly one of fear, doubt, and negativity, we mainly hurt ourselves. If our lives are dominated by hate, it is in that sea of hate in which we are forced to live. Segregation in the American South hurt those on both sides of the economic and racial divide. Maintaining separate schools, bathrooms, eating areas, and other facilities was in itself an expense, and the public coffers required the funds of everyone to keep services running.[61]

Many wealthy oligarchs try to deprive minorities of their voting rights and keep workers from making economic gains. Both in democracies and autocracies these oligarchs have a common intent: to maintain power by suppressing human rights. They dismiss the dignity of the people from whom their profits flow.[62]

If we want to live in the spirit of democracy, we might ask ourselves about our circle of acquaintances. Does it include only people who look and think like us, or have we expanded our circle to include those of different backgrounds who might challenge our limited worldview? Are we willing to push past our horizons to seek a more comprehensive understanding of those around us? Expanding our limits to include more people and their views can make our world a safer and more comfortable place.

Overcoming autocracy, although never easy, only is a part of the road to democracy.

More difficult is replacing it with a system that balances the needs of all. We may know what we don't want – poverty or division for example – but putting into place a fair and equitable society requires an ongoing commitment. Our leaders have an essential role in guiding our nations closer to, or further from, the implementation of that vision. Policies in autocracies mainly support those in power. The role of democratic government is to promote greater opportunity – in education, economics, vocational choice, and other areas – so that all can benefit from its commitment to equal treatment.

Although difficult, we can move our world in the direction of providing greater recognition of the rights and dignity of everyone. This begins in our individual encounters and extends to our governments. Segregation, mistreatment of minorities, and discrimination against women, although not eliminated, have improved as we continue to clarify our democratic vision. We can have a positive effect on the world – and ourselves – as we extend greater respect and opportunities to others.

It is easy to assign blame for what we see as the shortcomings of others and our world. Blame can be habitual, and always is non-productive because it leaves our issues unresolved. So when the question is asked: "Who do we blame?" the answers in keeping with democracy would be: "Why blame anyone?" and "How do we move forward toward solutions?"

When we judge others, we experience judgment. When we hate others, we experience hate. When we harm others or the world we make it less safe for ourselves. As we strive to make the world more fair and equitable, our lives also improve.

Two conflicting visions compete for our attention: dogma and democracy. Dogma is an inflexible belief that disregards evidence; democracy is a commitment to the vision of human equality. For those with low self-esteem, hating individuals or groups can provide a sense of temporary meaning, along with the comradeship of those who see the world the same way. When we move our judgments aside and see others as human beings like ourselves, we establish connections that strengthen our ability to move together toward common goals.[63]

Making this shift takes some self-awareness. When we see ourselves judging others, we can become aware of the harm that does to us and the world, and move from judgment to appreciation despite the flaws we all possess. That moves our minds from the realm of hate or criticism as we recognize the essence of others in the same way we want them to recognize us. It then allows us to move forward toward actions that benefit everyone.

If we decide that some people are more to be valued than others, that moves us back toward the autocratic vision by which humanity usually has been governed. But the autocratic mind never is satisfied; it always seeks to expand its influence and gain more control.[64]

If history is to be our guide, we can learn to move beyond the resentments and blame from our past to encounter each other anew.[65] This is the only choice that can preserve democracy. How we treat others is what we do to ourselves in the very moment we act.

### *Where we went wrong*

In both our personal lives and societies, we gave up our natural feeling of connection to others as we learned to emphasize our individual progress while ignoring the needs of those around us. This led to losing our understanding that mutual respect is what moves us forward.

### *How we get back on track*

The sense of connection we seek is something with which we are born and never goes

away. As we let ourselves return to that connection, we experience empathy for others,
the world, and ourselves. This affects our
actions as well as our mental state. It is the
essence of the democratic mindset that we
can bring to every situation at any time we
are not struggling to meet basic needs. The
alternative is seeing ourselves as victims bat-
ted about by fate. If we believe in democracy,
we support the rights and dignity of everyone
because if the rights of anyone is denied, all
are threatened, including our own.

# Third Guiding Principle of Democracy
## *Equal Justice*

Whent our societies became too large to function by consensus we needed rules and laws.

A primary difference between humans and other creatures is that we have morals, or ideals about how to act. Most of us believe that people should be kind to others and treat them as they would like to be treated. But that standard often is breached by all of us, intentionally or unintentionally. Thus we need rules and laws – that are rules sanctioned by society – to remind us of the behavior required to live with others. They address the difference between the world we would like and the one in which we actually live; the way we think we should act and how we really do act. Laws are needed to protect people when others refuse to abide by the commonsense rule of respecting the rights of those around them. This may be due to anger, a desire for personal gain, or simply being unaware or uninterested in the effects of one's actions.

Democracy is rule by all of us, rather than rule by one or some. Of course then there is the challenge of following our rules.

Anthropologists believe that in tribal societies there was an assigned intermediary to resolve disputes and no actual laws were needed. As tribes became states, laws, and judges to enforce them, were required.[66]

The first laws were oral agreements to create order in society, which eventually were written down. The Hebrew Bible was a tradition for hundreds of years before gradually being recorded on scrolls.[67] According to the book of Exodus, keeping order and resolving disputes was difficult until laws were put in writing, beginning with the Ten Commandments.[68]

Although there is variation among cultures – across countries and sometimes even within them – all known societies have established laws with the intent of ensuring justice among its members. These characteristically include prohibitions against murder, incest, rape, and regulations for the protection of property.[69]

In autocracies, the laws and their enforcement are skewed to favor those in power.

Rulers rarely are bound by law. Those who make and enforce laws in autocracies often are held to a different, more lenient, standard if they are held accountable at all.

Even when applied equally, laws can have unjust results. Many societies at one time imprisoned those who were in debt, or made them indentured servants with few avenues of resolution. The Athenians prided themselves on recognizing individual rights regardless of class.[70]

Laws are subject to the limited views of those who create them. The US Constitution, which claimed to be authorized by "We the people," was written largely by slave holders. It enshrined slavery and postponed the question of whether it could even be debated for twenty years.[71] By that time it had become more entrenched in the culture and economy of the South. The principle of treating other people as we would like to be treated was put aside for established custom and economic gain. The Constitution likely would not have been ratified without ignoring what many have called America's "original sin." Over time, laws in the US and other democracies have changed to reflect an expanding concept of human equality.

A review of a few US Supreme Court

cases demonstrates a growing understanding of what it means to protect human rights. The *Dred Scott* decision (1857) upheld slavery in the case of an escaped slave. In *Plessy v Ferguson* (1896) the Court allowed state segregation laws to continue despite the post-civil-war Fourteenth Amendment by claiming that separation of the races did not violate "equal protection of the laws." But by 1954, the Court ruled unanimously, in *Brown v Board of Education*, that "separate but equal *educational* facilities for racial minorities is inherently unequal," which began a long struggle to end segregation. In *Loving v Virginia* (1967), the Court ruled, again unanimously, that state laws banning interracial marriage violated the Fourteenth Amendment. And in *US v Windsor* (2013), the Court held that laws banning same-sex marriages violated the Fifth Amendment.

Those we choose as legislators, and those who become judges, must have demonstrated that they are committed to the principle of equal treatment. This means they support the view that the rights of the common person are to be upheld against those who wield financial or political power. They must demonstrate they understand that the right of individuals to make choices and control their own lives is paramount, except when their actions threaten or hurt others.

Laws generally prohibit harmful behaviors, rather than describing how people should act. Reasons for laws and their enforcement include punishing those found guilty of crimes as well as creating deterrents. But laws don't recognize that every situation is different. There often is an imprecise relationship between the intent of a law and its execution. Every crime is different; each involves different circumstances and usually different people. Every murder is different, every robbery is different, and every traffic violation is at least a bit different. Even where there is a genuine attempt at fairness by those who create or enforce laws, there is a variation in prosecution and penalties, depending on the severity of the offense and the view of the enforcer. There also can be special circumstances – such as accidents or lack of intent – that justify apparent breaches. That is why courts are needed to determine whether punishment or restitution is appropriate. Even then, different judges may rule the same case differently.

In democracies there is an assumption that justice is blind, although reality often falls short. People with wealth are able to hire top lawyers to defend themselves, but those who can't afford legal representation – often members of minorities – are most likely to have their cases poorly represented, resulting in convictions that might have turned out otherwise. Then there is the question of intentional or unintentional prejudice. The US – the world's incarceration leader – has a population of two million prisoners. Black men are six times as likely to be incarcerated as Whites, and Latino men 2.5 times as likely. If our goal is to reduce the number of prisoners and return them to society, retraining in vocational and interpersonal skills is essential.

This leaves us with questions about whether equal justice even is possible. How do we find a moral compass among the conflicting views that would guide our actions? How do we write – and interpret – laws that are most in keeping with democratic values? Is it possible to apply laws fairly when there are many disparities in interpretation and enforcement? Perhaps for guidance we should look to the views of some writers who have influenced our ideas about justice and morality.

Baruch Spinoza wrote his *Tracticus Politicus* in 1677, a prelude to the Enlightenment thinkers who influenced the American Revolution. He stated that laws can be put in place by common consent to protect the freedom of the average person from infringement by others. He believed that just laws are consistent with a consensus based on the morality inherent in a society.[72]

In his *Discourses,* John Jacques Rousseau discussed "the equality that nature has ordained between men, and the inequality that they have introduced." He tells us that in our original state of nature we were equal, but we have since created inequality, similar to the idea of lost innocence we find in creation tales, such as that of the Garden of Eden.

In his classic *A Theory of Justice,* John Rawls stated that in a just society "The principles of justice are chosen behind a veil of ignorance. This ensures that no one is advantaged or disadvantaged in the choice of principles by the outcome of natural chance or the contingency of social circumstances." That means laws ideally are conceived and enforced without first knowing to whom they will apply.[73]

Amartya Sen at Harvard has written many books on the nature of justice. In *The Idea of Justice,* he states that "Democracy has to be judged not just by the institutions that formally exist but by the extent to which different voices from diverse sections of the people can actually be heard....The need to transcend the limitations of our positional perspectives is important in moral and political philosophy, and in jurisprudence."[74] He is saying that in order to create a just society we must look beyond our own perceptions to a more universal perspective, because we necessarily are limited by our backgrounds and the groups with which we identify.

Perhaps the most significant principle that sums up what these writers are trying to convey is that in a fair society the rights and dignity of every human being must be respected. In autocracy, government is by a portion of the population that mainly serves its own ends, often at the expense of others.

In democracies we take for granted our ability to lead our everyday lives without interference. What we consider basic human rights are quickly deteriorating in many countries, even where democracy once was established. In autocracies, laws often are made to restrict free speech and keep people from asserting their rights.[75]

Another cause of our dilemma of democracy is that, despite wanting freedom for themselves, many people fail to understand that for human rights to thrive we must support them for everyone. Instead, we often divide into factions rather than engaging in mutual support. To maintain our own liberty it must be accompanied by our devotion to that of others. Claiming my rights and ignoring yours creates a situation where the rights of all are threatened.

The documents that came out of the American Revolution declared that basic rights apply to every human being. This idea was followed by the 1789 Declaration of the Rights of Man and Citizen after the French Revolution.[76] No clear direction for how to guarantee those rights was agreed upon by those who overthrew the French monarchy, nor by those who overthrew them, leading to an eighty year fluctuation between republic and autocracy.[77]

Eventually the Universal Declaration of Human Rights was forged by members of the United Nations in the wake of the destruction of the Second World War. Human freedoms began to improve with their economies. But soon a division occurred between democratic nations and those entrenched in autocracy, especially China and the Soviet Union.

The limits of my liberty end where I make your world less just. Laws can be made in the spirit of democracy, or of autocracy, to either create a society with greater justice and human freedom or to entrench oppression.

Democratic laws only provide protections if we follow them in spirit as well as in letter. In democracies, it is the responsibility of the majority to defend the rights of minorities because often they can't defend themselves.[78]

Within democracies, there are those who fail to treat others with dignity, often members of groups who they consider inferior. Police often are accused of unequal treatment of laws. They would benefit from training in how to move beyond their prejudices, which we all have. This hopefully would align their actions more closely with the principle of equal treatment.[79] [80]

In democracies the rights of all to participate in their religion is honored, but when religious beliefs include discrimination, the right of everyone to be treated equally must take priority. The US Constitution prohibits the government from establishing a religion. Belief in the superiority of one's religion or group cannot justify discrimination, but must yield to the principle of equal treatment under the law.

No one really wants to live in a world of hate and divisiveness. Seeing others as the enemy is not our natural condition, but one that can occur from blindly following others rather than developing our own sense of values. When we confuse our labels for people with the reality of who they are, we fail to see the person in front of us. By simply interacting with an open mind we get a much more accurate understanding of others.

Just as countries can grow in their understanding and establishment of greater human rights, each of us can expand our appreciation of each other and of laws based on affirming human equality, especially when we know they have been created to further the common good.

### *Where we went wrong*

We often seek justice for ourselves while ignoring its importance for others. Our understanding of others is based largely on the categories into which we place them. Thus it is human to judge. But as we force our world into categories, we become compelled to live in a world based on judgement.

### *How we get back on track*

It also is human to put our judgments aside and look at others with fresh eyes as we acknowledge our common humanity. When we realize that we all are valid individuals we bring an understanding of equality into our laws and everyday lives. When we see that our own justice only is secure as we guarantee it for everyone, we will have moved closer to a just society for all.

# Fourth Guiding Principle of Democracy

*Commitment to Truth*

Democracy is built on the truth of human equality.

From the time people began to think of themselves as separate individuals, they set goals and sought the best way to achieve them. They learned to put aside impulses so that their actions could build on lessons from the past.[81] Their ability to hunt and engage in warfare improved. With the advent of language – then writing and symbols such as those of mathematics – they could pass lessons on to others and future generations.

Knowledge has practical value that directly affects our lives. As our model of the world becomes more accurate, so does the likelihood we will act in a way that enables us to thrive. But each step toward greater understanding requires letting go of ideas that no longer work.[82]

Our decisions and actions are governed by our concepts, which may not always correspond to the real world. What we consider to be truth is a compilation of information accumulated throughout our lives.[83] We learn primarily in two ways: through direct encounter with our world and from ideas we get from others. If we learn from experience that bees sting, we will avoid them, or if we are told or read that bees are dangerous, we will be cautious in our encounters. If we experience that a person is friendly – or that another is not – we will act toward the first in a way that is trusting and act toward the other with caution. If we are told or read that a person or group is good or bad, the beliefs of others may become our own. Our beliefs then will determine how we view people, which may cause us to miss much of the reality in front of us.[84]

Our concepts can save or destroy us. If they become too rigid, they no longer will correspond to the people or world around us, causing us to misjudge them, or perhaps consider them threatening when they are not. Thus we must base our views on evidence rather than just on what we are told. As we understand the limits of our judgments and move them aside, we come closer to who and how people are. Beliefs about the superiority of individuals or groups are not based in reality.

Our ideas of the world must continually be revised to fit new information if they are to serve us.[85] Many people have beliefs that are so entrenched they are unwilling to change course even when repeated evidence contradicts their assumptions.[86] Some of us not only have a point of view, but we become our point of view, so we consider any disagreement to be a personal attack.

Our views are affected by the beliefs with which we are raised. If we are brought up learning to judge people, that will influence our perspective. If we are raised to accept a variety of people and behaviors, we likely will be tolerant of those we encounter. If we are reared in a religious household, we may believe that the world is divided into good and evil, or that everything will be transformed by a savior in an afterlife. A non-religious background may lead us to think that this world is the only one we ever will know.[87]

Those educated in democratic norms learn to value freedom of speech for everyone, including those with whom they agree and disagree. History and current events are taught in a way that encourages students to come to their own conclusions. But students educated in an autocratic system learn they are expected to believe and do what they are told. This is the case in many countries that once were democratic, but now have turned autocratic.[88]

Even in countries that consider themselves democratic, education does not always provide the skills to become responsible citizens. Parents or teachers may refuse to allow students to consider a variety of views that would inspire them to develop their own ideas. Banning books and conversations prepares students for autocracy. Censoring student input fails to train them in critical thinking, which is the ability to consider many options in coming to one's conclusions.[89] This is an essential skill that the US founders used to clarify their values and cooperate toward the creation of a democratic nation.

Schools – and societies – keep students from reaching their potential when they impose a standard of perfection rather than doing what is required to help them develop skills. When we judge students instead of inspiring them to learn, we cut off their natural curiosity and impose an autocratic mindset. Everyone is capable of learning if teachers respect them and their abilities. Rather than emphasizing what students don't know, we can help them improve their self-confidence and competence by building on what they do know from their experience in the real world.[90]

The proper role of education in democracy is not a race to see who can get to the top. It is an attempt to inspire students to reach their maximum potential, both as contributors to society and to their own welfare. Democracy requires an educational system that prepares learners to bring the principle of human equality into their daily lives; to think about which ideas and actions are in line with democracy and which oppose it. Schools fail students when they neglect to present them with a balanced view of historical truth.

When they emphasize pure academics, schools neglect to impart skills that are essential in daily life. Training in communication with others, the dynamics of raising a family, and managing one's finances are overlooked to the detriment of those who find themselves lacking competence in these areas.

In addition to educational and vocational choices, we all want to be able to speak freely and make the everyday decisions that affect our lives. Those who live in democracies may be unaware that such choices are denied for people in autocracies. The vast majority of societies have had rulers tell them what to think and how to act. If we want to live in a democracy, we need to know what we believe, why we believe it, and how to defend it. Otherwise others will do our thinking for us.

Leaders in Russia, China and many other autocracies distract people from their oppression by focusing on so-called "enemies of the state," both without and within. Wealthy oligarchs who support autocratic rulers dominate, while upward mobility is not available to most. But the wealthiest among us can be the most lonely and isolated because of limited everyday contact with other people.

The reason autocracies ultimately implode is because they and their leaders become more divorced from truth over time. Autocratic leaders choose advisors who tell them what they want to hear as they ignore feedback from the real world. During the current invasion of Ukraine by Russia, Vladimir Putin apparently only hears from advisors who fear to inform him that the war is going poorly for Russia. Putin is trying to recreate the Soviet Union, which failed because it imposed a series of disastrous plans while ignoring feedback about what is needed to be responsive to the needs of its people.[91] And he now is supported by autocrats from around the world including China, Eastern Europe and the United States.[92]

Democracy – although potentially the most satisfying political state – is harder to sustain than autocracy. It requires a devotion to learning how to think and act based on evidence rather than what we are told. It mandates ongoing dialogue to determine which actions best serve everyone. Autocratic leaders discourage dialogue and independent thinking because they want us to believe they possess the truth.

Even within democracies, some leaders will do all they can to tilt policies in their favor. The public easily is seduced by promises of leaders who oppose the basic democratic principle of cooperation for the common good.[93] Supporters fail to realize that unfettered freedom for some leads to that of others being compromised. This is likely to have negative consequences for all, including those who support these ideas and don't think through how they may limit their own freedom.

Most of us would agree that there is a reality – or truth – out there and that people hold widely different views of what that might be. Democracy is based on trust in people to come to their own ideas about what is true and to cooperate toward how best to put that into words and actions that serve everyone. A democratic voting system is based on faith that we can come to our own conclusions about our direction while keeping in mind the principle of equal treatment for all.

Balancing individual needs with those of society is not easy. Revolutions often result in new leaders who become tyrants. Reforming democracies by voting and activism is much easier and likely to succeed.

Reality is broader and deeper than our concepts, which, if we keep an open mind, always are evolving. Scientific understanding has developed slowly. Aristotle dominated Western science for nearly two thousand years before observations by Copernicus and Galileo began to replace his law that the earth is the center of the universe. Newton discovered the laws of universal gravitation, but the theories of Einstein superseded them by challenging the idea of an objective reality. Most great discoveries, such as DNA, have occurred where free inquiry was welcome.

What we think is true at any point in time will at some point be eclipsed by new discoveries. But our current views, based largely in the past, provide us an anchor by which we function. Awareness of our limitations provides a humbling lesson in how little we really know, and forces us to open to new possibilities. We remain dominated by the past until new ideas gain general acceptance. Thomas Edison struggled for years with models of the light bulb, and then an entire electrical network was needed to accommodate that invention. Automobiles required a series of filling stations before they could be of practical use. Electric vehicles have been slow to be accepted while awaiting the development of charging stations.

New ideas – no matter how brilliant – are accepted only when they have been shown to work better than those that were previously held. There always are those who refuse to acknowledge scientific progress. Most people accept vaccines for smallpox, polio and flu that are known to save lives. But in the midst of a long Covid-19 pandemic, many remained skeptical about vaccines and refused them. Relying on the best science available – although it may be far from perfect – is more likely to improve or save our lives than relying solely on beliefs. In democracies we have a right to refuse treatments or to participate in progress that might move society forward. Regardless of our beliefs, we have a responsibility to avoid behavior that threatens lives or impinges on the freedom of others. If we choose to ignore the benefits of science, we must stay out of the way of those willing to accept them.[94]

Our thinking – and actions – can be based on a short-term view of what seems right at the moment, or on a long-term view of what best serves everyone. Democratic political systems, and the science that is part of them, are based in continual revision by incorporating the best new information available. Autocratic leaders often keep themselves in power by disregarding the best science that benefits the public.[95]

There always are those who will tell us they have the truth and thus we should follow them. Their disciples seem unaware that truth never is concentrated in one person or political party. Truth only begins to be revealed after a long period of observation that is objective as possible.[96]

The role of the media in democracies is to provide information, not to tell people how to think. Some media hosts aim to provide a perspective about which leaders and countries promote democracy and which are autocratic. Others have become advocates for autocrats and seek to turn their followers away from democratic norms with partial truths and distortions of reality.[97] Media outlets often tell viewers what their sponsor wants them to hear. Some pundits have become expert at presenting a false picture. It is essential that people in democracies consider a number of views while coming to their own ideas about what is true. When we allow others to do our thinking we are on the edge of giving up our freedom. Media in autocracies uses misinformation to get listeners to support their distortions of what is true.[98]

In our minds we carry ideas about the past and hopes for the future. We may believe that the past was better, or the future will bring the world we want. But all we can do is focus our efforts in the present on bringing democracy into play in our personal and political lives. Our future will be dim if we fail to support its essential truth of human equality. Our struggle will have been worthwhile if we affirm our commitment to that truth, which is an essential element of democracy for current and future generations.

### *Where we went wrong*

What we know is limited to our concepts, which we tend to believe are the truth. Inflexibility keeps us stuck in the past and makes us unable to work with others on the essential task of preserving our democracies. Those who choose the autocratic path, and close off the conversation, imperil democracy.

## *How we get back on track*

We acknowledge that there are many valid views of what is true and what works. We get closer to truth by looking past our preconceptions as we observe the world around us and engage in dialogue with others, relying on science based on observation by many people over a long period of time. The essential guiding truth of democracy is human equality. It mandates that we interact respectfully with others while acknowledging their essential humanity.

# Fifth Guiding Principle of Democracy

*Protecting our Environment*

What we do to our environment we do to ourselves.

There has been a balance between people and their environments for most of the time humanity has been on the earth. This was recognized by our earliest myths and traditions. What we took from the earth we eventually put back, including our own bodies. In the Bible we are told: "By the sweat of your face you will eat bread till you return to the ground, for out of it you were taken; you are dust, and to dust you shall return."[99]

For much of our past we considered the earth to be not just our dwelling place, but a sacred asset essential to our well-being. Early hunters/gatherers were in awe of the power of nature and often evoked the spirits of animals as guides. Their activities were intended to bring them into alignment with

their surroundings as well as provide suste-
nance.[100] Starting about 30,000 years ago, cave
paintings began to appear in Europe, perhaps
indicating that early humans sought commu-
nion with the now extinct herds upon which
their lives depended.[101] Mountains often were
considered dwelling places of the gods. It was
from a mountain that the god of the Israelites
delivered their laws.[102]

Somewhere along the way we began to
think we could advance ourselves at the
expense of others and our surroundings. We
turned our backs on the damage we caused
and tried to move on. Eventually our damage spread so far and wide that it began to
have serious consequences on our ability to
function.

When we were in harmony with our environment – and other people – we were able
to sustain our world and selves. But when we
attempted to dominate all that is about us –
by war or exploitation – we endangered ourselves and gradually left greater expanses of
our planet unusable.

Beginning with the Industrial Revolution
in the 1700s, a deadly haze permeated the air
in London and other large cities. People's lungs
– and even their buildings – were infused with
soot and grime that shortened their lifespans.

It is impossible to leave a trail of damage on our planet without it catching up to us and affecting our own health and prosperity.

The basic problem, and the solutions to our environmental dilemma, are easy to understand when we reduce them to a scale we readily can comprehend. If we were to live on a very small island with only a few inhabitants, we would need to combine our efforts for the benefit of everyone. Abusing our environment by overcutting or burning down trees, overhunting, overfishing or depleting the soil would have an immediate effect on our surroundings and our welfare. Looking after our individual needs while ignoring those of others, rather than working for the common good, would lead to suffering for everyone.

Human beings started with reverence for the earth that sustained them. But since then we have failed to respect the environment upon which we depend, and the effects of our actions on others, in our inexorable march toward what we mistakenly consider progress. We now are on the verge of creating conditions for ourselves and our planet that only can be corrected by concentrated and coordinated effort by everyone.

For those who pay attention to science, there is no doubt that human activity has been the major contributor to our environmental degradation.[103] Just as we might believe in the golden rule, but often fall short, we have failed to show determination to address this major crisis in a unified way. An obstacle to our working together is the lack of unity and determination among those of us – that is all of us – who have created the problem. It will take an adjustment in our lifestyles and a new determination to act in unity to eliminate planetary desecration.[104]

What stands in our way is an inability to combine the efforts of everyone worldwide to focus on solutions. Only when people are able to meet their basic needs can they begin to consider larger issues. There is a part of humanity that is struggling at a subsistence level and has no inclination to look at the consequences of their actions. So dealing with international poverty must be included in our approach.

Another major obstacle to moving forward on our environmental emergency is the autocratic mindset that exists to an extent in all countries, where profit is prioritized over health. But environmental degradation affects everyone at all levels of society.[105]

In his book *Collapse*, Jared Diamond points to some of the reasons that people have failed to act in a coordinated way to prevent their own demise: "It turns out that societies often fail to attempt to solve a problem once it has been perceived...some may reason correctly that they can advance their own interests by behavior harmful to other people.... Unhappy outcomes include the overexploitation of most marine fisheries, and the extermination of the megafauna (large animals, birds and reptiles) on every oceanic island or continent settled by humans....If the elite can isolate themselves from the consequences of their actions, they are likely to do things that profit themselves, regardless of whether their actions hurt everybody else."[106]

Some areas in which actions engineered by human beings threaten our health and future, and some potential solutions, follow below.

**Global warming** is the most urgent threat to the continuation of life on our planet. It is caused largely by our pollution of the air around us.[107] Our daily activities in modern society include burning fossil fuels as we create pollutants that warm our atmosphere. Among them are ground and air transportation, heating our homes, methane production from the manufacture of materials such as steel or cement and from raising cows for dairy and meat, and the application of chemicals used as fertilizers.[108] Global warming already has caused the deterioration of Artic and Antarctic ice and increased incidents of wildfires worldwide.[109]

**Water pollution and shortages** threaten us as we fail to protect this precious resource. The problem is made worse by the heating of the planet that warms the ocean and threatens its ecosystem, including the fish we eat and all ocean life. Factories and agricultural runoff discharge pollution into rivers and streams, threatening typhoid and lead poisoning, and killing animals that live there. Even more than household consumption, "farms, factories, highway medians, and golf courses" use the bulk of water in our society.[110] According to one article, "Ageing infrastructure, legacy pollution and emerging contaminants across the US are driving a growing urgency to do something about America's water crisis."[111]

**Plastic pollution** is increasing as we use more plastic bags and other products that clog large and small bodies of water, as well as harm fish and birds that swallow those items unaware.[112]

**Pesticides and chemicals** are poisoning our food and land that becomes unusable as it is overfertilized, causing a waste of land that cannot be reused.[113]

**Rising seas** caused by melting glaciers are threatening coastal areas inhabited by those aware of the problem and even by those who deny it. Low-lying island nations already are disappearing.[114]

**Abuse of resources,** such as overfishing and overharvesting our forests, has resulted in depletion of these assets upon which we depend.[115] [116]

Bringing an awareness to society of how our actions can lead to destructive ends has been, and continues to be, an ongoing challenge. When automobiles first were developed, no one thought they would lead to serious environmental problems. Smoking cigarettes in public places was common until the toxicity of cigarette smoke was acknowledged. Because the effects of our pollution threaten our very existence, we need to engage in a universal effort on a massive scale. As we have become more aware of the destructive potential of some of our most ingrained habits, we are beginning to see a willingness to change.

Judges in the US are demanding a climate impact analysis for drilling projects, and in some cases are cancelling oil drilling leases.[117] [118]

New industries are being developed to mitigate the effects of pollution on our planet.

Research is being done on capturing carbon from the atmosphere.[119]

Types of degradable plastic are being produced and more nations are working together to eliminate the problem.[120] [121]

Alternative fuels, although long being developed, are at last showing that they can make a viable contribution to reducing greenhouse gasses.[122] Even airlines are developing engines to use sustainable fuels.[123]

Investors in large corporations are voting to discourage the use of fossil fuels. The pressure is being felt by many companies and banks. [124] [125]

Electric vehicles, although slow to capture the public eye, now are a booming industry. There currently are thirty types of electric cars available to consumers in the US.[126]

The dangers of pesticides to human health are being recognized by our courts.[127]

Finland has set an example for the world and has mandated that all of its energy sources be renewable by 2050. [128]

The state of Illinois, once a bastion of heavy industry, now has created a clean energy coalition to recommend ways to move to less environmentally-threatening means of energy production.[129]

Many people fear that they will lose their

livelihoods if their government forces a switch from polluting to sustainable fuels. But moving to a green economy opens up many opportunities for those who are willing to undergo a minimum amount of training in sustainable fuel industries.[130]

Each of us also can reduce the use of resources as we develop more planet-friendly practices and limit our consumption. The use of electricity in the US is increasing, which stresses power grids and leads to increased outages.[131] We may not be aware of how much we consume in the course of everyday living. Almost everything we use affects the viability of our planet because it consumes energy at every step enroute to us. Even vegetables are grown with fertilizers and then transported to our stores, where they are placed in coolers; that involves three carbon intensive steps before we consume them.[132] It is up to our government to set standards to prevent resource depletion. We should be hearing from our leaders about specific ways we can prevent waste.

To reduce pollution and lessen global warming, we each must make individual contributions to a more viable planet. Here are a few questions we might ask ourselves:

*Is this something I really need?*
*Must I shower every day?*
*Can I use less electricity?*
*Can I eat more locally grown fruits and*
*vegetables?*
*Can I wear a sweater rather than turning up*
*the heat?*
*Can I wear my clothes longer without washing*
*them?*
*Can I take public transit rather than driving?*
*How can I weatherize my home?*
*Do I really need a house with six bedrooms for*
*a family of four?*[133]

Dr. Hari Lamba, in his book *Brighter Climate Futures*, outlines a number of ways we can reduce pollution by more sustainable practices. Non-polluting sources of energy include solar, geothermal, hydrogen and ammonia storage fuels. Other ways to reduce the use of carbon fuels include electrification of buildings, redesigning trucks, planes and ships to use nonpolluting engines, and developing carbon sinks by growing more forests and limiting deforestation. As individuals we can mitigate the problem by installing solar panels on our roofs, purchasing energy-efficient appliances, composting organic waste and traveling in energy-efficient ways such as trains. We can prepare for the effects of climate change that already have begun by saving more rainwater via underground cisterns, using desalination plants, and changing agricultural practices to adopt to lower water use. He also discusses how countries with the largest populations, including China and India, are far behind western democratic nations in reducing their carbon output. Since what happens in one country affects the others, western democracies must support other nations in efforts to mitigate an ecological disaster that only can be prevented by international cooperation.[134]

We have gargantuan issues to address. We will not solve them by focusing on who is wrong. The state of our environment is so urgent that we cannot let ourselves be distracted from our need to give the problem our full attention.

### *Where we went wrong*

At some point we decided to go to war with our environment, not realizing that by doing this we harm ourselves. We function under an illusion of endless resources, while much of the world remains chronically short. Democracies are divided within themselves about how best to acknowledge and mitigate the threats to our planet brought on by our lifestyles. Some people stick to their beliefs – often based on what they are told rather than evidence – regardless of scientific consensus.

### *How we get back on track*

Scientific truths often take a long time to become established in the popular imagination.[135] The dangers of smoking took many years of publicity before it prompted protective action, and this still is not the case around the world. The threats of our everyday practices to the viability of our planet now have been established by reams of scientific evidence collected over years. Armed with those facts, scientists, and every one of us, must push legislators and industry leaders to protect the environment that has sustained us since life began, and that we now threaten to destroy along with our own lifestyles and planet.

# Sixth Guiding Principle of Democracy

*Fair Elections*

Fair elections are the basis upon which democracy is built.

The idea of electing the leaders of a state was initiated in Athens in the sixth century BCE. Full citizens, perhaps ten percent of a population of 300,000, could participate in meetings of the Assembly that debated and created the laws.[136] They elected their top ten officials, including the military commander, and drew lots for distributing administrative positions.[137]

Rome became a republic about the same time. Two consuls who served simultaneously were elected by popular vote for only one year, and it was their duty to preside over the election of their successors. Livy's *History* reflects the pride which with the Romans regarded their freedom, or *libertas*.[138] Rome lost its free elections when the Republic was replaced by an autocracy in 27 BCE.

In the unsteady march toward modern democracy, there were stirrings of citizen assemblies among the Vikings and medieval republics in Novgorod (now part of Russia), Hungary and Poland.[139]

In England, the beginnings of Parliament took place after the signing of the Magna Carta in 1215. Parliament met once yearly, or less, through a long period of contention with the Crown. When Charles I was overthrown in 1649, the Commonwealth was established under Oliver Cromwell that became another autocracy until his death in 1658. Charles II was reinstated as king by an election in 1660, but then he ignored Parliament. The 1689 Bill of Rights laid the foundation for parliamentary sovereignty, but the long struggle between Parliament and Crown continued through the 1800s. The Reform Act of 1832 gave the right to vote to about seven percent of the population. Property qualifications for men were abolished in 1918, but women did not win the right to vote until 1928.[140]

The New England colonies began a struggling existence with 104 English men and boys seeking adventure under the Virginia Company, which was financed by investors. They founded Jamestown in 1607, named after

King James I. Fifty-one settlers died of starvation and disease within six months, but the local tribes helped them. Another ship arrived that included two women the next New Year's day. There was no incentive for hard work as they labored under a taskmaster of the overseas company, and the colony almost collapsed. It was saved when land was allotted to the settlers who then could profit by planting tobacco. Voting rights for males were initiated in 1619, after which they elected the first legislative assembly in the colonies under English Common Law. Democracy, with its essential right to vote, had come to America.[141]

The Puritans arrived in Massachusetts on the *Mayflower* in November, 1620, seeking religious freedom from what they considered the rigidity of the English Church. About half of the 102 on board were adventurers with no interest in religion, so a clear agreement on governance was required. This resulted in the *Mayflower Compact*, signed by 41 men from both groups. About half of the settlers starved that first winter, but were helped by the local natives under Massasoit, with whom they signed a treaty in which both promised not to "injure or do harm to any of their people."[142]

Before the 1776 Declaration of Independence, voting qualifications varied between colonies. In general there was a requirement that only male landholders could vote, but because land was readily available, about 75 percent became voters. After the revolution, most of the states reformed their voting requirements to allow all taxpaying White males to vote, although with religious requirements for some, as they ratified their state constitutions.

With the failure of the 1777 Articles of Confederation to create a unified nation, representatives from all thirteen states attended the Constitutional Convention in Philadelphia in 1787. The resulting Constitution was worked out as a compromise by delegates from the states after four months and sent back for ratification. It was – and is – a testament to the fact that people of varying views can reach agreement on a forward-looking document. Its stated intent was to acknowledge the rights of all, despite its many shortcomings and those of its signers. Some delegates quit or refused to sign. The rest put aside their differences to create a Constitution that was signed in convention on September 17, 1787.

The ratification process took place in special elections in each state. Approval by nine states was required before the Constitution could become law. There continued to be considerable opposition. The ninth ratification, by New Hampshire, didn't come through until June of 1788, and that of Virginia followed. Because the state conventions required popular input, the ideas in the proposed Constitution were discussed among a broad segment of the population. Qualifications to vote for delegates varied, but New York waived its property requirement and allowed all free males to participate.[143]

The US was the first country to have regularly scheduled elections. In the election of 1789, George Washington basically was acclaimed as President and John Adams became Vice President. In March 1790 both were sworn in. The last state, Rhode Island, didn't ratify the Constitution until later that year. The "more perfect union" they formed was a binding agreement that prohibited subsequent exit.[144] The Electoral College, mandated in Article II, was based on the distrust of some framers of the popular vote.[145]

Then, as now, there were those in favor of "government by the people," and those who opposed it. A large portion of the country understandably had no concept of democracy and wanted a new king, with many fleeing to Canada to remain under the Crown. James Madison, as did Plato and Socrates before him, had doubts about self-government for fear of a tyranny of "passion over reason," or the majority over a minority.[146] So Madison authored the Bill of Rights, which was certified as the first ten amendments in 1791.

George Washington declined a third term to avoid turning the presidency into a monarchy. In his *Farewell Address*, which was a 32 page letter to the nation, he warned of the dangers of allegiance to political parties rather than to the democratic principles of the US founding: "The spirit of party...is a spirit not to be encouraged." By resigning he affirmed his belief that allegiance in democracies must never be to individuals.

In New Jersey, the state constitution gave the vote to "all inhabitants," with unforeseen results. During a hotly contested election in 1806 for a seat in the legislature, men, women, boys and girls all voted, and twice as many votes were cast as there were voters. The results were cancelled and the legislature passed a law that those allowed to vote had to be free White men who either owned property or were taxpayers. By the Civil War there was universal White male suffrage in most states.[147]

Since that time, the US has undergone many revisions in its determination of who is worthy of the vote. Many other countries have had democracies temporarily, and then lost them, with a receding number where genuine democracy – respect for the principle of the sovereignty of the people – still exists. Autocracy has triumphed where meaningful voting has been curtailed. Only in countries where the bulk of the population understands and honors democratic principles has it been maintained.

Within all democracies there is a struggle about how best to take into account the rights and needs of everyone as we each pursue our own rights and needs. We often must choose to base our votes on what we consider our narrow interests or on the wider interests of our society.

Voting to install leaders who uphold democratic principles greatly influences our lives. We are affected by whether our laws – and their enforcement – are designed with a balanced view of the needs of all, whether there is equality in educational opportunities, whether there is fair pay for one's work, whether there is adequate healthcare to treat us and return us to productive lives after injury or disease, whether our chosen lifestyles are protected,[148] whether we are allowed to follow our beliefs that don't interfere with the rights of others, and much more. Bringing the principle that "all are created equal" into the everyday lives of people will have implications for each generation beyond what the previous generation could have imagined.

Real democracy requires that all adults are allowed to vote in elections, with the possible exception of those who are removed from society for crimes. It mandates that all votes are counted toward the results. People have a right to refuse to vote, but laws that impede voting violate the basic democratic principle of treating people equally. Rigged elections are the realm of autocracies and those who support them.

In elections there always are winners and losers, so it is essential that votes are fairly counted and that there is a system in place to monitor them to the satisfaction of all sides. If people lose faith in elections – as has happened in a number of once democratic countries – they are of no value. The election outcome must reflect the actual votes and, in the US, be aligned with the electoral system. And then the loser must concede.

Democracy in essence is a willingness to put oneself in another's place so that everyone's rights are protected. Government by the people requires finding and acting on common ground for the mutual benefit of all. "Life, Liberty and the Pursuit of Happiness" for only some cannot be guaranteed unless the objective is to assure those qualities for everyone. Our votes – and those leaders we elect into office – must be guided by those principles. Looking after the needs of only oneself or one's group is what preceded democracy and is what still guides the autocrats of today. This has resulted in mass inequalities which have caused insurrections throughout history and that will continue to threaten autocracies wherever they exist.

When people believe that their leaders work against their interests they often have engaged in rebellion, which usually has been put down, sometimes brutally. The American Revolution came very close to failure. After successful rebellions, people hope to reestablish their basic rights. Where democratic governments have been established, individual rights have been protected for most, but not everyone. The hope in democracies is that the will of the people will be heard as elections replace revolutions.

Because we want security and stability, we are willing to give over a great deal of our decision-making to leaders. But when leaders no longer focus on the needs of the people as a whole it is time to replace them. This is done in democracies by elections that have been established in the wake of revolutions.

Elections must remain fair to maintain their validity. We must work within the system whenever possible, because when we over-turn it we may bring on something worse, as often has happened.

To preserve democracy, voters must assess leaders based on whether their actions move them closer to – or further from – the principle of equal treatment for all, regardless of polit-ical party or promises. Patriotism is a com-mitment to the principles of democracy, not to a leader or political party. Real democracy is not just voting; it is a lifestyle. It is borne of mutual respect and support among people, which is the guiding principle in the constitu-tions of all nations, although some countries only use their constitutions as window dress-ing as they deepen their autocracy.

In some democratic systems, voters directly elect leaders and in others they vote for political parties. No system is inherently better. To be democratic, elections must be based on the widest representation of adults possible. Where votes are suppressed by legal or other means, the stage is set for the votes of everyone to be discounted.[149]

When threats and violence to overthrow a legitimate election become acceptable, we have turned to the same playbook as Russia,

China, Poland, Turkey and all other countries where elections have been manipulated by eliminating competition and establishing one party rule. Without fair elections democracy is dead. A viable democracy depends on competition between individuals and parties dedicated to the principle of fair play. This includes acknowledging the will of people in elections. Political parties and leaders who support violence to overturn elections are more interested in winning than maintaining democracy.

Democratic representation also has practical implications for our everyday lives in our communities. I live in Oakland, California, and have been asked to weigh in on local issues, such as whether trains with loads of coal will be allowed to traverse our city, or if we should allow homeless people in recreational vehicles to park on our streets.

Those who safeguard fair elections should be honored for their essential contribution. To ensure fairness, elections must be monitored by representatives of opposing candidates or parties who review the results together. Those who attack election officials are attacking democracy itself.[150]

Issues about the fairness of elections exist in countries around the world, particularly in those with a history of autocracy. International monitors are required to ensure that the results are based on the actual vote.[151] [152] People in countries with democracy have an obligation to support it wherever it exists. Allowing democracy to disappear anywhere is a threat to its existence everywhere.[153]

### *Where we went wrong*

Many of us welcome free elections and assume they are guaranteed to continue. But democracy is threatened by those who seek to keep themselves in power rather than adhere to the principle of fair elections.

### *How we get back on track*

When we vote we must accept that we – and the people and issues we support – may win or lose. Holding elections that include all adults, and counting their votes by representatives from all sides, is the only way to ensure that all are counted and that fair elections remain in place. When we overlook rigged elections in other nations or our own, we are setting the stage for the deterioration of the standards of fair representation everywhere. That is why election procedures must be subjected to monitoring by bipartisan representatives of democracies.

# Seventh Guiding Principle of Democracy

*Freedom of Choice*

The freedom of everyone is intertwined.

In democracies freedom has a special meaning. Our choices must be balanced with our responsibilities to society. People of a democratic mindset think about the consequences of their actions to others and adjust them accordingly. They are aware that freedom only is possible with a structure to support it. Freedom is not about being at odds with others and our environment. It is understanding who we really are: individuals connected to the world around us. Freedom only can be experienced in the context of that connection.[154]

John Jacques Rousseau wrote in *The Social Contract* that although people are "born free," authoritarian governments leave them "everywhere in chains." He believed that the path to protecting the individual requires that members of society participate in a voluntary "contract" in which everyone recognizes the rights of all.[155]

Competition can motivate us. But when competition becomes a life and death struggle, democracy is threatened. Democracies are about providing equal recognition and opportunities for everyone. This is the only way to maintain stability; it is when the phrase "all are created equal" becomes meaningful. Freedom requires rules and laws that protect our right to make the major decisions that affect us. Without structure we revert to being a society where the strong dominate the weak, which moves us in the direction of being "in chains" once again. When laws favor the few, rather than the many, it may be time to challenge them. This is the standpoint from which the American Revolution was launched.

We often think of our rights as being absolute. But they are founded either on a common vision of mutual respect, or on an assumption that only our view is correct. Rigid beliefs – not reality itself – cause our polarity. Our views – and our actions based on them – fall short of a full understanding of the world and the reality of others. No one knows the entire truth; we need to be suspicious of those who say they do. When based on the assumption of human equality and free enquiry, democracy melds many perspectives to bring us our best approximation of truth at any point in time.

What is most important in democracies is that we listen to each other. This is how we expand and improve our views and make our actions more effective in the real world. We often think we must win or lose, that our freedom is exclusive of that of others, but when we take this view both we and democracy lose. We have much more in common than we have differences. In the case of abortion, for example, we may choose to use the label "fetus" or "child" for what a pregnant women is carrying, which leads to ideas of absolute right and wrong. To reach resolution in this and all other areas, we need to move beyond the dichotomies we ourselves create and look at the reality of each situation as we seek solutions.[156]

There always has been – and always will be – individuals and factions that try to gain control of democracy under the guise of freedom. In Athens there were oligarchs who conspired to use democracy to snatch control for themselves.[157] Julius Caesar tried to move Rome from democracy to autocracy before being assassinated.[158] Huey Long was a populist

American leader who abused his power to override democratic norms and was assassinated in 1935.[159] There have been many leaders and countries who use terms like democracy and freedom to make people think they are protecting their rights as they restrict them.[160] This also is a tool of some politicians who don't like the way they are portrayed in the media and then threaten the press.[161]

Autocratic leaders take absolute views that don't consider the reality of many people and situations. They surround themselves with "yes" men and women as they become more divorced from reality. They close themselves off to feedback from others, including their followers, and ignore the needs of those they are supposed to lead. That is why so many people seek to escape autocracies.[162]

In democracies, who is right or wrong is not as important as actions that consider the humanity on all sides. A hard stance on rights makes it impossible to seek a solution that takes the interests of all into account. Democracies are based on equal enforcement of laws, built on the idea of the value of every human being. At one time courts in the US affirmed the importance of a common path to individual rights.[163] In Europe and elsewhere courts often emphasize a middle ground.[164]

In democracies we have an obligation to assist those who have fallen behind to restore their confidence and competence. This can stabilize the economy for everyone and could take many forms, including counseling or vocational training.[165] People only can make the important choices that affect their lives when they have a sense of stability. This may be a long path, as many have fallen into poverty or self-defeating behaviors, but if we choose a world where some forever remain behind we also are in danger of falling behind if our own supports fail. Many would rather complain about the poverty and homelessness they see around them than work to improve those conditions.[166]

Those of an authoritarian mindset believe they become free by blindly following their leaders. Hitler and Mussolini both came to office by democratic means, but once they had the trust of their citizens began to strip them of their rights. The same has happened in a number of former Soviet republics; Russia, Poland and Hungary among them. In our day the Russian Bear threatens the independence of its neighbors, even those that have become more autocratic in recent years. When an autocratic power threatens, the most effective action is to distract it by strong measures before it actually attacks.

In democracies there are endless choices that people are accustomed to making. These include educational and vocational decisions, what to eat and wear, getting the best possible health care, determining where or if to worship, whether to have children, whether to drive a car, which gender role to assume, whether to carry a gun, choosing to consume recreational drugs or alcohol, and deciding to protest if we feel neglected by our government, among others.

There also are choices that have a potential to harm other people. Among these are smoking cigarettes, refusing to take vaccines that protect us and others, driving through a stop sign, violent protest, and speaking in a way that incites violence. When our choices negatively affect others we are acting beyond the range of legitimate freedom. Democracies are justified in prosecuting those who are a danger to society.

As we claim our freedoms, we rarely stop to think that for those not living in democracies – which is a growing majority of the world – making choices is a luxury. The only way to maintain the right to make responsible choices for ourselves is to do all we can to ensure them for everyone, everywhere.

To provide a clearer picture of what would be lost under an authoritarian regime, imagine if you were not allowed to make the above choices. The educational system dictates that what will be taught is aligned with the authoritarian views of the government, you are told what vocational direction you are allowed to pursue, your food and clothing choices are determined by what the government approves, the number of children you are allowed is dictated by the state, there only is a source of poorly made cars available, you can be arrested for minor infractions that require paying a bribe, you can be put on trial for false charges where the jury is instructed to find you guilty, your alcohol and drug choices are limited by the state, public protest can land you in jail or cost you your job.

The needs and rights of everyone in a society are connected. We survive only with the assistance of others. Interdependence – for both our physical and emotional needs – is a fact, and the more we acknowledge it the more fulfilling our life is likely to be. This is the essence of the democratic view. The autocratic view sees democracy and freedom as a threat and wants to control or eliminate them. Autocrats support each other in their quest for domination. Those who seek expansion are threats to the continued existence of human freedoms.[167]

When autocrats threaten democracies, it is up to leaders to communicate clearly that world domination fantasies are not acceptable. Waiting for attack is inviting it. Once an attack begins it is much harder to curtail. Before World War II, Hitler expected the world to react as Germany began to swallow its neighbors, but Western democracies at first encouraged aggression by doing nothing.[168] During the 1962 Cuban Missile Crisis, John F. Kennedy did not wait until missiles were housed in Cuba and aimed at US cities – he sent a clear message that threats are not acceptable by setting up a blockade, during which the world held its breath. Democracies represent the best interests of everyone, and are justified in taking the offense when incursions are threatened. This route is much more likely to head off danger before it builds strength.[169]

In the Cold War era, democracies broadcast democratic perspectives to countries behind the Iron Curtain by use of a network called *Radio Free Europe*. It brought hope to millions who were suffering oppression. Although it is being repressed in authoritarian countries, it still can be broadcast using alternate channels to reverse misinformation and inform those under oppression that democracy is alive and in support of them.[170] If propaganda media like *Russian Television* wanted to broadcast into democracies, that should be welcome. China also has released a paper called *China, Democracy that Works*. Encouraging those living in democracies to debate alternative views would allow them to develop critical thinking about what does work and what doesn't to sustain democracy.[171] This would open an exchange of ideas while bringing up legitimate questions about how it could improve.

Countries that are democracies in name only – including Russia, Turkey, Hungary, The Philippines, Nicaragua and now Hong Kong[172] – have rubber-stamp advisors, legislators and courts. Any sign of independence, freedom of speech or self-determination is extinguished. People live in fear of doing or saying anything in opposition to the regime lest they be whisked away to jail, tortured, or worse.[173] In the case of Russia, dissidents outside the country have been killed.

Within countries where people consider their governments democratic, some autocratic leaders have large followings. They twist the truth by using vast generalities about minorities and others. They focus on blame rather than possible solutions.[174] Those of an autocratic mindset are comfortable with leaders who demand absolute obedience and a political party that seeks to eliminate fair elections and equal opportunity. But by supporting these leaders they undermine their own freedom.

Democracy is not a gift. It is a luxury we must earn by continual monitoring and action to ensure that our leaders have not embarked on the autocratic path. Free expression and choices that do not harm others must vigorously be defended. Countries that become democratic after throwing off autocracy – like those of the former Soviet Union – have no tradition of democracy. They need guidance from democratic countries about how to maintain their freedoms. The victors of World War I failed to provide support for the losers and imposed draconian reparations. The predictable resentment was a factor in the emergence of an angry Germany and its authoritarian leader twenty years later. Support in rebuilding then was done successfully by the victors after World War II. But the world's democracies have failed at more recent opportunities to do just that, which has created an opportunity for autocracy to return.[175]

If we have learned anything from history, hopefully it is that democracy always must be defended, even in our conversations, and that human rights must be upheld everywhere. Democracy represents the ideal of accommodating the views and needs of myriad individuals, and it must be committed to the defense of people who hold those views – or who act on them – short of harming others.

## Where we went wrong

In Western democracies many people take their freedom for granted. They often express what they consider their freedoms as absolutes without taking the rights of others into account. They assume that their right to live freely never is seriously threatened until they see that the threat is real, as has happened with recent invasions of republics like Georgia and Ukraine.

## How we get back on track

While democracies stand for free speech and toleration of all views, those living in them must recognize speech and actions that threaten the freedom of others. Autocratic leaders should be sanctioned by those who support democratic values before threats build to a critical level. We must promote democracy whenever possible by engaging with others in respectful ongoing dialogue to move past our dichotomies toward common solutions.

# Eighth Guiding Principle of Democracy

*Shared Prosperity*

An economy that really works benefits everyone.

From the time there have been people on the earth there has been a division of labor within families and tribes. Some would hunt and procure food, while others did domestic chores like childcare, weaving, or basketmaking.

The economy of every civilization began as trade – first between individuals, then between tribes, then in markets, and eventually between nations. Money at first was a way to store value that could be any durable small object such as shells. The main criteria for money was – and is – that all users agree to its value. Evidence of trade in early European cultures goes back three thousand years.[176]

The archaeological record shows that the earliest societies were mostly egalitarian. But as civilizations grew, and rulers became more distant from their subjects, greater inequality began to appear.[177]

The history of inequality includes serfdom and slavery throughout Asia, Europe, Africa, and later, the Americas. Groups that conquered others, such as the Aztecs, sacrificed war prisoners,[178] and ancient Greeks enslaved those from other city-states they conquered. African tribes enslaved other tribes.[179] When people accumulated debts – often farmers – they sometimes lost their freedom after a series of bad harvests. Thus debt has long contributed to inequality. Debts can facilitate positive economic flow that benefits the lender and borrower, but economies come to a halt when debtors no longer can keep up.[180] As has been documented in many civilizations, debt forgiveness has allowed economies to rebound from stagnation.[181]

When prosperity was based on the exchange of goods and services, there were good times and bad, depending on natural causes like weather events or human-caused crises like invasions. In our modern international money-based economy there is a large amount of debt between individuals, institutions, and governments worldwide. So when economic flow is interrupted, it can create cascading effects on nations and have global repercussions.

Severe financial downturns have been recorded several times every century since the General Crisis of 1640, which was the result of a period of civil war and unrest in Europe. The reason for most downturns is a huge amount of debt that cannot be paid back, which then causes investments to fail. Governments have created new policies in the wake of financial crises to prevent future crises, but putting regulations in place often has not been effective because of failure to seriously enforce them.[182]

In the US, the South tried to secede from the Union during the Civil War to retain its economy based on the practice of slavery, which was incompatible with democracy. There have been many other regions and countries that have sought to establish independence in the hope of preserving their cultures and end what they considered economic domination. Some have been successful, including the original American colonies, former Soviet republics leaving the Russian Federation, and Algeria leaving France. Others have not been successful, such as the attempt of the South to leave the United States, Basque and Catalan regions to leave Spain, and Chechnya to leave Russia. In our modern world economy, the interdependence of all regions and nations means that economic ties will at some point be renewed, after sanctions or even wars. Whenever possible it would work best for break-away regions to negotiate how to maintain ties while keeping their identities, rather than to risk their economies by a creating disunity. The people who live in these areas must be consulted if such efforts are to succeed.[183] Basic human rights considerations always should guide such negotiations.

The democratic mindset of human equality slowly has gained traction since the American Revolution. By nature, we tend to identify with those we consider like ourselves, and less so with those we think of as different. Tribalism exists in the mind of every human being. Moving toward shared prosperity becomes more difficult as the interests of one group supersede the needs of everyone else. But when we support economic flow to all levels, it benefits everyone, including ourselves.

Money has no intrinsic value. It represents the goods and services we can exchange for it. Only in rare periods of difficult economic times – such as the Great Depression of the 1930s – did some people store the bulk of their funds on their own premises and keep them out of circulation. Some of the most wealthy of our day keep a portion of their funds "off shore" to avoid making their contribution to society, and according to current laws, this is "perfectly legal."[184]

Those who hope to accumulate wealth – which is most of us – deposit funds in banks which loan them at higher interest than they pay. We may think of our money as being safely deposited, but it actually is circulated to others, creating considerable wealth for banks and not nearly as much for depositors. It is similar in stock markets, where invested money is used to expand businesses. When things work well, there is a circular flow of funds from individuals to banks or businesses and back to individuals that keeps economies moving.

During financial downturns, everyone is affected, but those at the lower end of the economic scale are hurt most.[185] In the Great Recession that began in 2008, there was a considerable increase in hunger and many lost their homes worldwide. Those at the top, however, were able to survive comfortably until the economy came back.[186] Many banks benefitted from government bailouts that were intended to support those in need, but often instead created bonuses for those who lent out money they received at zero interest from the government. Banks also seized homes in foreclosure that they then could resell. But the ultimate source of government funds is the taxpayer. After that downturn, reforms were put in place by the *Dodd-Frank Act* of 2010, including a requirement that housing loans must require 20% down, and raising the "stress test," or the level of reserves that banks must retain. As can be expected, wealthy interests have been trying to eliminate that act.[187] It was partially repealed in 2018.

Downturns threaten the financial stability of everyone, and recovery never is assured. What works best to maintain prosperity for everyone is ensuring a flow of funds between those at all economic levels. When this happens, the vast majority of people have enough to maintain their lifestyles, but businesses also profit when they provide what people want to buy. When more people are impoverished, less revenue is generated for businesses. Those who most affect the status of the economy are the non-wealthy because there are many more of them and they put most of their income back into immediate circulation.[188] To allow the economy to improve in a way that benefits everyone, there needs to be job training available for those who have lost work or want to improve their situation.

This is where governments can participate in public/private partnerships to bring greater prosperity to the bulk of people.

Most economic research shows that general prosperity benefits those at all economic levels. That view also is in keeping with the vision of the US founders that government in democracies is by and for "We the people," not some of the people. It was famously elucidated by President John F. Kennedy in a 1963 speech where he stated: "A rising tide lifts all boats."

There are economists who base their conclusions on political philosophy, backed by those of great wealth, rather than on what works in the real world. Their backers have invested great sums in moving us toward an autocracy where their interests dominate, and in recent years they have had considerable success.

The University of Chicago was founded in 1890 by John D. Rockefeller, whom economists agree was the richest man in history. He had a monolithic empire built around Standard Oil in the early 20th century that was broken up in 1911 under antitrust laws.

It is no surprise that the *Chicago School* has become known as the bastion of conservative economics.[189] Among its associates were Friedrich Hayek and Milton Friedman who both championed what became known as "libertarian" views that have contributed to an autocratic tradition which greatly influences American politicians and judges. This has tilted much of American law, and its enforcement, toward a view that serves the interests of the most wealthy at the expense of the rest.

Hayek, an Austrian economist, in his most well-known work, *The Road to Serfdom*, claims that social planning is socialism.[190] His view is understandable, considering that his book was written as Hitler and his National Socialist Party nearly destroyed his native Europe while Soviet Socialists dominated much of Eastern Europe. But these were not socialist states, they were authoritarian dictatorships bent on ruling the world. Hayek doesn't deny that some protections are needed to foster competition that is compatible with democracy.[191] Libertarians who claim Hayek as a hero oppose the worker protections he mentioned, as well as the social service system he tolerated. The version of Hayek's "Definitive Edition," published by the University of Chicago Press, makes extensive comments in footnotes throughout the book, but ignores this essential element of his view.

Milton Friedman, the most famous disciple of the *Chicago School*, deservedly received the 1976 *Nobel Prize in Economic Sciences* for his contribution to monetarism, which emphasizes the importance of government controlling the money supply to avoid extreme downturns. This is in contradiction to the free market philosophy he espoused in his books.[192] The essential view of free market economists is that markets should be left alone and everything will be just fine. But leaving everything alone has led to slavery and children working long hours in factories. Letting market forces prevail has led to the autocracy that inspired numerous revolutions, including that of the American colonies. Among the other obvious examples of the shortcomings of that view are the *Great Depression* of the 1930s and the *Great Recession* that began in 2008, both of which required legislation to rein in a runaway financial sector.[193]

By contrast, John Maynard Keynes, probably the most famous economist of the 20th century, wrote his **General Theory of Employment, Interest, and Money** in 1936 during the *Great Depression*. He proposed that governments can lessen or end downturns by borrowing money and pumping it into the economy, a view that now has become standard wisdom, and which brought relatively quick ends to the *Great Recession* that began in 2008, and the downturn that began in 2020 as a result of the Covid-19 pandemic. This practice has been used in the US by both Republican and Democratic administrations, and in European nations, to good effect. Keynes also proposed changing tax rates to stimulate or slow the economy as needed. Once those measures succeed, he advocated letting the "classical economics" of competition come back into play.[194] He believed in government intervention only when needed to stimulate a stalled economy.

Autocrats put aside the larger picture of what best serves everyone to gain greater control under the guise of patriotism. In Britain, people voted in the 2016 Brexit referendum to sever ties with the rest of Europe that brought them prosperity, having been wrongly convinced that the European Union is a threat to their sovereignty and would cost them millions of pounds yearly.[195]

In the US, there is a collusion of some of the most wealthy that have convinced people to oppose real democracy in the name of freedom. The book *Democracy in Chains* describes how a Koch Brothers funded cabal invested years – and millions of dollars – in efforts to overthrow the structure of American democracy. In 1976, Charles Koch bankrolled a "think tank" to spread the view that unfettered free markets enhance democracy. A real think tank is devoted to reaching conclusions based on evidence, not pre-ordained views. The Cato Institute, as it became known, was and is committed to challenging every organization that supports the infrastructure of democracy, including public schools, the postal service, minimum wage laws, child labor protections, and foreign aid. Its ultimate goal is an end to taxes and any type of government regulation on business.[196] Koch-Funded organizations, such as the Heritage Foundation, promote "school choice" and criticize what they call the "lies" of government officials during the Covid-19 crisis on their websites.

Such organizations are not about public service or freedom. Their quest for control is based on unlimited funding from the wealthiest individuals to influence legislators and courts about "libertarian" ideas.

Media plays a huge role in influencing how viewers think about politics in their nations. The Rupert Murdoch media empire has become a major source of indoctrination. From *The Times* in London, to the *Wall Street Journal* and *Fox News* in the US, to the *Australian News Channel*, much of what he supports, particularly by his editorial boards and commentators, is autocracy under the guise of democracy.[197] This is similar to the tactics used by

*Russia Today*, the constant drone of misinformation that is the primary source of news for Russians, and which was used as a propaganda source to justify the invasion of Ukraine.[198] Real democracy is a threat to oligarchs, whose pundits dutifully reframe autocracy to make it sound democratic, and democracy to make it sound oppressive. Many viewers are unaware they are being manipulated and fail to seek balance in their media input.

Corporations are created to serve people and generate profits, which are not necessarily contradictory. Corporations are not people who should enjoy legal protections, and laws regulating them should reflect that reality.[199] If free markets really worked for the benefit of all, we wouldn't have needed an American Revolution, or any other revolutions, to reestablish the principle of human equality. The so-called "libertarianism" of a Frederick Hayek or a Milton Friedman or a Charles Koch is designed to liberate only the elite at the expense of everyone else who must pay taxes to uphold the infrastructure of society.

For those coming from a tradition of privilege, including some White men in Western culture who believe themselves threatened, a society where everyone is treated equally is unacceptable. Thus the chant at violent rallies that "Jews (or Blacks or Asians) will not replace us." This is the desperate plea of those who, for the most part, are economically insecure and claim racial superiority in an effort to gain recognition and security.[200] But their leaders have neglected them under a guise of "freedom." Government incentives are needed to help those who see themselves as abandoned to find training in skills that will build their futures and self-esteem so they no longer feel compelled to attack others. Retraining programs are a way that the supports of democracy can work as intended.

Those who insist on unlimited freedom – and profits – for themselves to the detriment of everyone else never can have enough, because such views are the result of isolation from others, not deprivation.[201] No amount of money can cure that compulsion. But efforts to raise living standards by democratic governments – which represent and benefit all of us – can restore our faith in democracy and ourselves.[202]

### Where we went wrong

Some claim that unfettered competition brings prosperity. History shows that this only is the case for those who end up on top.

Prosperity for some at the expense of others divides society and keeps everyone struggling against each other.

### How we get back on track

It is the role of all of us in democracies to support each other to reach our potential throughout our lives. Then we will be able to contribute to an economy where we all benefit. If the choice is between a situation where everyone wins and just a few win, our path should be obvious.

# Ninth Guiding Principle of Democracy
*Standing up for Democracy*

**D**emocracy cannot survive on its own.

To keep our democracies in place, we must go beyond words to actions that protect them from both internal and external threats. From the perspective of our everyday lives it is difficult to see how we fit into history. When the future looks back at us will we be remembered as a generation that sustained democracy, or let it die? And if democracy disappears in our time, will there be anyone to write its history? Much of that depends on our actions in the present.

It is natural to assume that our society and world always will remain the same. But a glimpse at history shows us that no civilization is everlasting, including those of ancient Egypt, Athens, Rome, the Middle Ages, the Renaissance, and many others since that time. The democracy that some hold dear, and others take for granted, will likely be of short duration unless we identify – as individuals and nations – what we must do to keep it, and then act on what we have learned.

To successfully confront autocracy, those who believe in democracy must be proactive, not just reactive. That means we confront monolithic thinking wherever we encounter it. When people – or nations – show obeisance to a person or political view that ignores the value of every human being, we don't just give those views a pass, but challenge them by pointing out how they threaten us all.[203]

At the time of this writing, the biggest European battle since World War II is being waged by Russia against democracy in Ukraine, which most nations considered stable until recently. A little more than twenty years ago, Russia was seen as moving toward becoming a democratic country. But it has no such history. It was an empire created out of smaller states that conquered others by a tradition of ruthless wars, including the conquest of Novgorod, an assembly of free citizens who were slaughtered by Ivan III (known by Russians as "The Great") in 1478.[204] When Russia seemed to move toward democracy after the 1991 fall of the Soviet Union, Western democracies did little to help establish a viable economic system and way of life. Oligarchs confiscated what once was state property while many Russians did not have enough to eat. This gave democracy a bad name.

In a 1956 speech, Nikita Khrushchev, Premier of the Soviet Union, announced to the Western world: "We will bury you!" Now Vladimir Putin, once a member of the Soviet Secret Police (KGB), lacking Communist ideology but armed with an autocratic mindset, has made it clear he wants to reconstruct the Soviet Union. This is a war on democracy itself and all it represents. Western powers allowed him to get away with bombing civilians in Georgia in 2008,[205] and Syria in 2015,[206] as well as jailing dissidents and killing opponents who escaped abroad, without serious repercussions.

The parallels to the beginnings of World War II are impossible to ignore. The European powers gave Czechoslovakia to Hitler in 1938 to prevent war when he claimed to defend the "oppression" of Germans living there. With the exception of Winston Churchill, they failed to read Hitler's true intent of world domination.[207] Russia invaded Ukraine in 2014 under the pretense of liberating Russians in the country. When democracies fail to stand against autocratic expansion they encourage and embolden further attacks.[208]

It is essential that democracies confront the incursions of autocracy everywhere they exist, and as they occur. This is best done by coordinated efforts. Autocracy seeks to feed upon others and engorge itself as it consumes all it encounters. If democracies are to stand for human rights and equality, a series of gradually more crippling sanctions, and possibly other consequences, must be imposed whenever and wherever they are threatened. This should be done before the worst aggressions occur, because wars are much harder to stop once they start. Democratic powers must respond strongly because the language of autocrats is aggression. We can observe, complain, criticize, and document the abuses of the autocrats of our day, but until we act strongly to curb those abuses, they will continue unabated until they overwhelm us. If we really want to preserve our way of life, action cannot wait until that happens.[209]

Countries that invade others must be expected to provide retribution for their damage. Knowing this will be required might provide a disincentive for attack. This must be done while the economies of both countries are being rebuilt to avoid the mistake of impoverishing the loser, as was done to Germany after The First World War, which sparked its wish for revenge.

Some might believe that confronting auto-cratic nations could lead to a nuclear conflict, but the aggressions they already pursue put everyone at risk. We need to decide whether to submit to fear or stand for the rights of those who are oppressed and attacked, and ultimately of everyone, including ourselves. Where attacks on innocent civilians are sus-pected, an international tribunal should be invoked.[210]

There are people who think that when there is a war in other places between dem-ocratic and authoritarian forces, we are not threatened and therefore should not be con-cerned. But all democracies are vulnerable to attack and must stand together in defense.

Now imagine what an attack might look like by an autocratic power that seeks world domination. It would not need to be a phys-ical attack to be crippling. A cyber-attack could shut down our food, water or power supplies, empty our bank accounts, or make our payment systems ineffective. We need to be aware of this real possibility and support those – usually in our government – who have the never-ending task of combatting auto-cratic aggression.

After the 2001 attack on the World Trade

Center and Pentagon, the US and its allies went after its perpetrators. That effort extended for 20 years and kept the US embroiled in the Middle East. Serious mistakes were made, including toppling the government of Iraq in 2003 under the pretense of upending "weapons of mass destruction" that never were found. In Afghanistan, the beginning of a return to democracy was begun in 2004 with a constitution and elections. This was continually challenged by the Taliban and others. Their main goal was to return to controlling the country under strict and intolerant Muslim rule inconsistent with the views of most Muslims. Nevertheless, this was a foothold for democracy under which residents breathed the air of freedom until abandoned by the West in 2021.[211] The situation now is dire with rights obliterated and many starving.[212] When the US abandoned efforts to maintain democracy in that country by withdrawing its remaining 5,000 troops, the message was clear to many that democratic countries no longer would stand for universal human rights.[213]

If we are to live in a world where human dignity is respected, then we must confront autocrats in democratic countries as well. They already have come to power in many previously democratic nations like Poland and

Hungary, and threaten real democracies with so-called populist movements in France,[214] the United States, and many other countries.

On January 6, 2021, supporters of President Donald Trump attacked the US Capitol Building after his speech telling them: "If you don't fight like hell, you're not going to have a country anymore." The result was extensive damage to the Capitol and five deaths. Members of Congress had to flee for their lives. Both Republicans and Democrats immediately condemned the attack as well as the speech that inspired it. This clearly was an organized effort because insurrectionists participated from across the US. Compliant Republicans now excuse the attack as actions of "ordinary citizens who engaged in legitimate political discourse," and condemn their prosecution.[215]

If democracy survives in the US, the history of this insurrection will show that the rioters and those who support them are traitors. But if autocracy takes over, they will be seen as heroes. When members of a major political party legitimize an attack on democracy, they make it clear they no longer support their Constitution or the rule of law. This is a step on the road to tyranny. In the book *How Democracies Die,* the authors state: "Democracies may die at the hands not of generals but of elected leaders – presidents or prime ministers who subvert the very process that brought them to power."[216] To their credit some Republicans are willing to stand against the insurrection and acknowledge its threat to democracy.

The concept of universal respect and the actions of democracies toward others often are not consistent. They have a history of subjugating people under the guise of liberating them. Colonialism perpetuated by Western democracies controlled over 80 percent of the globe in 1914, and only ended in the 1970s, but the idea that Whites of European descent are superior to everyone else persists.[217]

When we penetrate the veil of many democracies to see the self-interest pursued by those who claim to live by its principles, the contradictions between what people say they believe and what they do becomes apparent. The concept of "We the people" is easy to state but difficult to bring into play in our lives and governments. That phrase must apply to individuals at all levels of society. If we are to act in a manner consistent with democracy, we must extend respect to everyone while making it clear we stand together in preventing human rights abuses everywhere.

## *What individuals can do*

For democracy to succeed, we must act in a way that demonstrates its vision of human equality. Because we are creatures of habit, we need to practice this in our interactions.[218] Opening our hearts and minds to others is beneficial to us and might even make our own world a better place. That doesn't mean we trust those with a history of abuse of others or democratic principles, but if we dwell in a state of continual fear and opposition we mainly hurt ourselves.

To live in a democratic world we must treat others, even those we consider opponents, with the recognition and respect we want. We cannot know for sure, but perhaps if the worst human beings we can imagine of the past and present were given the human recognition they wanted, our world would be a better place.[219] Hatred toward others may or may not affect them, but it definitely has a negative effect on us. We may believe that our views are superior to others, but that does not make us superior human beings. The belief by some that they are better than others provides them permission to dominate, or even eliminate, people. Once slavery – then segregation and discrimination – were considered normal, as were anti-gay and anti-immigration views. Depriving any people of their rights threatens equal treatment for everyone.

A commitment to respecting human dignity leads to actions by which we can become instruments of democratic ideals. In our daily conversations we will encounter views that are autocratic; where people claim the superiority of some. Without insulting another person we can confront the idea that an individual or group is superior by simply pointing out: "I don't think that view is compatible with democracy."[220]

Vladimir Putin currently is pressing a narrative that Ukrainians are Nazis; therefore subjugation and even elimination is justified. We have seen this excuse of blaming the victims throughout history. It can be difficult to admit when our group does it to others. Protecting human rights is not an area in which we can afford to be reticent. Imagine if those who hid Jews during World War II declined for fear of the consequences. We either are for or against human rights, which means the rights of all, and we must have the courage to back those views.[221]

When we allow our conversation to regress into which person or group is superior or more deserving, we enter the realm of autocracy.[222] When we commit to the principle that all are equally valid human beings, we bring that view into our interactions. Maintaining democracy requires bold and continued advocacy by those who believe in it. Everyone can't be a politician, but everyone needs to be political to preserve it.

When we see misinformation coming from leaders, the media or others, we must question what they are saying and refuse to be caught in any suggestion that people or groups are better than others. We can confront these ideas by use of conversations, meetings, demonstrations, letters to politicians or newspapers, or any other means necessary. Around the time of elections, we can encourage people to vote for leaders who represent democratic principles. This can be done by sending letters, going door to door or participating in phone banks.

The most significant feedback for leaders is whether they remain in office based on the votes they receive. It is up to us to evaluate whether politicians promote equal and fair treatment for everyone, and we should support those who do.

We also need to broaden our horizons by recognizing that those who don't look or think like us are as human as we are. Democracy is built on diversity. We or our ancestors all are from elsewhere. The contributions of immigrants to our lives and lifestyles should be honored. They also make a substantial contribution to our economy.[223] It is good that not everyone looks or thinks the same. This brings us closer to a more broad and democratic perspective.

There is one essential guideline to making our interpersonal communication about how best to bring democracy into our lives and world more effective and meaningful. We must continue beyond discussion to action if we are to make a difference. A determination to resolve issues is essential so that we create solutions that serve us all. It is only when we commit ourselves to creating and executing a common plan that we and our democracies move forward.

When our issues remain unresolved they become amplified in people's minds. This results in alienation, and moves us backward rather than forward. Commitment to arrive at a common understanding, and to implement a plan based on that understanding, made the difference between merely a destructive revolution and the ability of the US founders to forge a nation. It can be the model for those who want to move beyond discussion to effective action. When a plan consistent with human rights is approved by a majority, it should go forward even if some lag at getting on board.

## *What families can do*

At the level of the family we must prepare each other to be resourceful citizens ready to live in, and defend, democracy. Children can be encouraged to develop and express their own views, based on exposure to the real world when possible, rather than having the ideas of their parents imposed. Every child is an individual, endowed with a creative potential to contribute to society that can be nurtured and encouraged. It is essential to build self-esteem by letting children be as independent as possible consistent with their safety. If we believe in democracy, we see each individual as valuable, not because some are "winners" or "losers." We all are winners when we acknowledge and express our intrinsic worth.

## *What schools can do*

Schools can continue to build on the independence and skills begun in the home. This can be done by engaging students in projects of interest rather than imposing "subjects" that have no relevance to their lives. The questions we ask should encourage them to think and come to their own ideas about what is true and right, rather than imposing what adults think are "right answers." Education in democracy is preparing students to cooperate with others to achieve common goals that best serve them and the world in which they live.

## What organizations can do

My background is in teaching and health care management. My experience – backed by the views of numerous writers – is that employees perform best when they understand the goals of the organization and are given the freedom to work toward them based on their own initiative. Showing genuine appreciation for the contributions of employees is the key to motivating them. Feedback can be given in a way that is positive and builds rapport. It must be clear that actions – not personalities – are being discussed in an effort to help everyone work together toward common goals. Feedback heard as personal criticism will be resented.[224] Communication skills can be practiced and then brought into the context of everyday interactions. Employees must be monitored to ensure they are doing their jobs, but micromanaging impedes their ability to make their best contributions.

Beyond making a profit, corporations in democracies have a responsibility to be in accord with democratic ideals. Most large companies are global and subject to the pressures of many types of governments, including autocracies. If they operate in countries that promote falsehoods or oppression of some of the population, they are in danger of becoming part of that oppression. They cannot take a "neutral" stance toward propaganda meant to deprive people of their freedoms, and in some cases, their lives. They must refuse to participate in efforts by governments that harm people or lie to keep themselves in power.[225] Otherwise corporations risk contributing to the autocratic mindset that threatens us all.

### *What governments can do*

Democratic governments must advocate for the equal treatment of everyone under their wing and express concerns for governments that neglect the needs of their people. They must work together to forge a stance on human rights against the forces that oppose them without and within.

To promote greater rights across the world, democratic governments could rely on a scale that measures the commitment to freedom and equal treatment in all nations. Freedom House already has a similar Ranking of Democracies.[226] There also is a UN Human Rights Council, but it has no power over the actions of governments.

Countries could be evaluated by use of a ranking system about whether they meet essential criteria for human rights. Countries – and possibly leaders – could be ranked by an international committee that determines which nations fall to a low point on the scale. Those nations would be given the option of improving their record within a time limit, or experiencing gradually greater sanctions until their record improves. Sanctions ideally would be applied in a way that has minimal effect on residents and maximum effect on autocrats.[227]

Democratic governments also can use broadcasts to convey the voice of freedom to nations under oppression. If all outside information is cut off, leaflets can be circulated into countries to encourage those who may think they have been abandoned.

Those who enforce laws often are inadequately trained in the principle of treating everyone with equal consideration. Training of police in practice situations where they get to know and work with those they oversee

– particularly minorities – would help them see others as human beings like themselves whose rights are to be protected. Convictions for police misconduct are costing cities billions of dollars as juries become convinced they do not enforce the laws equally or justly.[228]

In the US many voters are excluded from fair representation in gerrymandered areas designed by politicians seeking to maintain their advantage regardless of how people vote. This has become a problem in states where legislators ignore democratic principles in order to stay in power. It represents a danger of overthrowing democracy itself, and it is up to the courts to confirm the principle of "one person one vote."[229]

The media in democracies is responsible for supporting "truth in broadcasting" to a public that depends on them for information. Since the advent of cable news, some networks cleave to a partisan line, promoting the views of autocrats at home and abroad.[230] As the independence of media in autocracies is being crushed, the responsibility becomes greater in democracies to present a balanced view. In the US, it is the role of *The Federal Communications Commission* to monitor stations to ensure they are not repeating lies promoted by autocrats. The 1947 *Hutchins Commission on Freedom of the Press*, created in the wake of World War II, outlined five criteria for the press to follow that would provide excellent guidance for our day.[231]

Governments in democracies must create regulations to protect the environment that supports life on earth. They should advocate for responsible treatment of resources to best serve the needs of the general population, rather than corporations represented by lobbyists who advocate only for the profits of their clients.

It is up to our governments to preserve the principle of equal opportunity across the spectrum of people's lives. In the US that is the job of the *Equal Opportunity Commission*. It also is the role of prosecutors to investigate crimes committed by members of one group against others for the purpose of expressing hate. State and local governments often are in support of local prejudices, so we must rely on a higher federal standard.

It is important to be sensitive to others and their perspectives, but the one view we can insist on is that, regardless of how wealthy or talented anyone may be, no human being is superior to any other. This can be the basis of our interactions in every type of situation. When we interact in our homes, with friends, in our workplaces and organizations, we must insist that no one is treated unfairly.

Mass action to resolve inequities can be

preceded by conversations between individuals and their leaders to reach a plan that takes everyone's rights into account. Autocracies can set objectives and move toward them much faster than democracies.[232] But autocracies only seriously consider the views of their leaders. If we are to demonstrate that democracies are preferable, we must move past legislative stalls to a clear plan on which we act, to show that we are responsive to the needs of those who require government intervention.

Even though we work together toward solutions to the issues that confront us, we will at times need to admit we fall short because we approach them with limited understanding, and no one knows absolute truth. We may need to take a break and then come back to consider new options with an ultimate commitment to resolution. The essence of democracy is that we all learn from each other and are guided by our experience as we seek the best solutions possible.

This process is in contrast to autocrats who claim to have the truth while refusing to consider a diversity of perspectives. This is why autocracies are of limited duration, the former Soviet Union being a prime example. It is likely that democracy will win out because it reflects faith in the talents and abilities of many individuals to come together. We will stumble often, but we then can rise again in our commitment to the truth of human equality as we combine forces and continue to improve our democracies.

## *Where we went wrong*

We often have failed to stand up for democracy as individuals, groups, or nations, as we gave up on reaching consensus due to the difficulty of cooperating with others to implement a common vision. Autocracies are attractive to many because they take that responsibility out of our hands.

## *How we get back on track*

Democracy is about universal respect for human rights. When it is diminished anywhere it is diminished for us all. Therefore, we must present a clear message that restrictions on rights by autocrats will not be tolerated, both within our countries and without, and that gradually more stringent consequences will result for those who violate them. Our goal is to move toward a world where all see for themselves that when human rights are respected it improves life for everyone. This is the most essential element of democracy.

# The Road to Freedom

In his 1863 Gettysburg Address, Abraham Lincoln envisioned "a new birth of freedom" rising from the ashes of the Civil War that took more American lives than any war before or since. Yet Lincoln – who recently had lost his own son – saw beyond the sorrow of the moment to a time when democracy would make everyone free.[233]

Lincoln also knew that the preservation of his nation required following a firm and clear path. He supported punishment or disciplinary action for those who violated that path, including insurrection or desertion, and dismissed one of his more prominent generals for disobeying orders.[234]

As the US founders were aware, freedom is not only about a break from the past, but mainly is about creating a vision for the future that best serves everyone. Those who fought the American Revolution were men of many races who forged a nation that became an inspiration for people everywhere. [235] [236] They overturned what they saw as oppression to bring themselves and future generations that freedom of which Lincoln spoke. But the descendants of some groups who fought in that war still experience discrimination in voting, housing, law enforcement and the way they are treated by their fellow citizens.

Our world faces many challenges to come together in the face of tyranny; to affirm the rights of everyone to freedom and fairness. The road is not an easy one, but if we are guided by a clear vision of human equality we will continue advancing toward that goal. We will be pulled off track by setbacks. Then we can choose to recommit ourselves and refocus individually, as groups and as nations, on the bigger picture of connecting with others for the common good. We can live dominated by disappointment, or continually renew our vision for what our world and lives might become. If we regress into pessimism we already are defeated in our thoughts, and the defeat of our aspirations will follow.

Our natural condition is to be social beings. We engage others in interaction from the beginning. No child chooses to be isolated. As we develop a sense of who we are, it always is in relationship to those around us. Only later – when disappointed in human encounters – some withdraw when they decide that others cannot be trusted.

In some countries there is a tradition of distrust. These are places where autocracy long has reigned and the rights of individuals are quashed. In recent years there have been millions of refugees who have risked their lives – and those of their families – to escape such oppression.

The state of the world always remains in play between those who seek to dominate others and those who cooperate to create the best world they can. Democracy stems from a sense of morality, its roots in relationships with those around us, where we see that the welfare of all is connected. According to Michael Tomasello, perhaps our day's most prominent researcher into human motivation: "Moral reasoning derives from children's empathetic engagement with others as they, in a sense, put themselves in the place of another and 'feel his pain.' "[237]

The pessimists among us say that history is the story of disappointment and we should resign ourselves to a world where human rights remain out of our control. Optimists say that although the path to freedom is filled with hazards and pain, that must not deter us from our democratic vision.

As I write, there is a war being waged by Russia on its much smaller neighbor Ukraine.

Ukrainian cities are being laid waste by an attack unprecedented in Europe since World War II. Yet Ukrainians and their president refuse to yield.

What is it about democracy and freedom that drives people to risk everything? Ukraine could submit to Putin, who has claimed it is part of "historical" Russia. Rather, Ukrainians struggle mightily to remain independent. And why did nearly every democracy on earth condemn Russia by imposing sanctions that also will hurt themselves, while removing Russians from posts everywhere, even in the arts?[238]

We started this book discussing how, within the mind of each of us, there is a side attuned to democracy, and another that prefers autocracy. We want freedom but also desire a structure to follow. The US Constitution – although flawed – was a statement of how both elements might live side by side. Its main author, James Madison, was concerned about human passion overwhelming the discipline needed to sustain democracy, so the Preamble tells of the structure needed to "create a more perfect union."

No one person or ideology has the last word on how democracy should look. The beginning of the end of democracy lies in trusting those who tell us they can lead us down that path. Putting our confidence in a person or political party, then looking away, is a sure route to losing our freedom. The only way to maintain it is eternal vigilance.

With democracy comes choices and responsibilities. There is no one absolute path, but only the guiding principle that everyone is created equal. That idea is difficult to put into practice in the real world. It is especially hard to understand for those who believe that some – usually they themselves – are superior to others.

Perhaps the roots of our dilemma lie in democracy itself. Perhaps the freedom wrought by democracy is too difficult a responsibility. Perhaps a need to create our own future is less important than the certainty of having someone tell us what to think and do. There are perhaps too many choices in democracy, such as finding and backing leaders who uphold democratic principles, rather than simply following those who will do our thinking for us. The burden of monitoring leaders is a task that most people would rather leave to others as they conduct their daily lives.

With all its difficulties, for those who believe in democracy, there only is one side. We choose the universal respect of human rights to ensure our own. We don't know what the ultimate picture will be; perhaps there only will be a continually changing and challenging world. We do know that cooperating with others toward common solutions is preferable to submitting to subjugation in thought or action.

The entire history of humanity can be summarized as a struggle between autocracy and democracy. This struggle continues every day in our personal and political lives. It is about whether to succumb to what we are told to believe and follow, or to take the less certain path where we consider for ourselves what is likely true and thus best serves us. The former is easier; the latter strewn with pitfalls.

A confrontation between autocratic and democratic forces is gathering. This is not the first or last time that these forces will align in opposition, but every moment affords us an opportunity and choice. We can cower in obeisance to our authoritarian impulse – whether from within or reflected without – or we can summon our faith in our ability to tread a democratic path.

The most famous saying of Theodore Roosevelt, US President 1901-1909, was "Walk softly and carry a big stick." If we were to update that for our day it might read: "Be kind and gentle whenever possible, but don't give an inch when democracy is threatened, or you might end up giving it all away."

The democratic road is based on determination to participate in an alliance that affirms the dignity of everyone. Its route will not always be clear, but we can be guided by a concept of making the world more livable for us all. If we are directed by a vision of what we are for, rather than what we are against, it increases our chance of success. By insisting on that light we create a model for those who equivocate. We make clear by our actions the truth of human equality. We lead our lives boldly – but not recklessly – in the confidence that this principle will guide our way.

There is a longing for simplicity in the human mind – for a return to a time of innocence that perhaps never really existed. We hope for a leader who will bring us back to that perfect world. We imagine it as a time when purity reigned and to which we can return by eliminating the impure elements of our world. This, however, is the part of us attracted to autocratic leaders who promise to create a perfection that exists only in our minds. This is when we become aligned with those who remove anyone who stands in our way. And this is when we sacrifice our sense of morality and justice to a totalitarian vision.

The opposite view is appreciation of all people, with their strengths and limitations. For real understanding we must move beyond our ideas about others and openly encounter the complex beings before us. We are much more than the labels we assign to others and ourselves. Who we are becomes better understood in our interactions, and includes an ability to simply enjoy the company of others in each new moment.

When we label people as the enemy, no dialogue is possible. If I see you as obstructing my fulfillment or happiness, eliminating you becomes justified. But we can move beyond being consumed by hate and blame. In the words of Lincoln, "we must disenthrall ourselves." This permits dialogue toward our common benefit, as was done by previous enemies after the second World War.

Our relationships enter a new phase when we attempt to create and move toward common goals. Communication becomes essential – whether in our homes, schools, organizations or nations. Words may not adequately describe the vision we hold in our minds, so continual communication about our plan to reach our goal is required along the way. And for some of our endeavors, such as maintaining democracy, the process will be ongoing.

This is the type of freedom for which we were born – to create a structure that ensures our ability to be free. In the anarchy of what some call "free enterprise," there is non-ending competition that leaves some on top and some underneath, but all struggling against each other. This is the belief under which some have fallen as they cast aside the basic tenets of democracy.

While dialogue is essential, it must be followed by concrete action based on agreements we have made to build the structures for our democracies to work. These structures must take into account the environmental emergency we have wrought that threatens our planet and lives.

There is a silent lonely place within each of us that seeks recognition. It knows that who we really are is not our looks or race or sexual orientation or vocation or group or level of wealth, but rather that entity at the core of our being and our true self, which is at the same time always connected to the world. This is where we started and long to return. It is the essential nature of each of us that loves all of creation and thus ourselves. This is the self we abandoned to assume the identity of a separate being. But our real self remains connected to our world, and we can return to that view via respectful interaction with all that is around us. As we show deep appreciation for others we experience it for ourselves.

Just as we have an innate ability to create, we have a tendency to judge. The first is required to move our lives forward, and the other is needed to gauge our progress. Our creativity is expressed in our daily actions and interactions. It also is a social process by which we create our societies. When the judgmental side of us stifles our creativity, an essential part begins to die. One might say that we can be our own best friend or worst enemy.

Democracies have no final form. They are agreements between those who create unique models of self-government. Autocracies – on the other hand – follow the form of government that their leaders impose. This is why so much of the greatest achievements of our past and present have taken place where human creativity was honored.

On March 4, 1865, Lincoln gave his Second Inaugural Address before a huge throng gathered outside the US Capitol. He intentionally kept it short, and rather than focusing on blame for the destruction of the Civil War, he emphasized the task of rebuilding. He demonstrated the attitude required for healing to take place: "With malice toward none with charity for all..."[239] The next month he was assassinated by a man who called him a tyrant.

We might wonder what Lincoln would think if he was able to glimpse at the progress of his country over 150 years after his death. He might be pleased that human rights have improved – slavery and official segregation are gone. But he might be aghast that many people still are legally denied the vote, in contradiction of his belief in "government of the people, by the people, for the people."

There always has been, and always will be, those who cling to their limited view of the world. They are unable or unwilling to focus on the big picture of how we can make our nations and lives prosper. But Lincoln always kept the vision in mind of a time when the nation would be reunified. He held those accountable who threatened society, but refused to dwell on blame.[240]

Lincoln had a number of conversations with Frederick Douglass, the great abolitionist. He earned the confidence of Douglass not only by his support for ending slavery, but also by the way he treated everyone with equal respect.[241]

So perhaps we can learn from the man whom those of many political perspectives consider the greatest American; that democracy lies not only in laws and their application, but in how we interact with each other. Hopefully we don't need to wait for yet more history to teach us to move beyond our preconceptions about others and treat them with the respect we want for ourselves. Perhaps we can begin that practice in our everyday encounters, starting in this very moment.

# For Further Reading

I have used a variety of references that support the views expressed in this book, and also some that do not, in the interest of maintaining a balanced perspective. I strive to consider input from publications, the media and other people that cause me to rethink and enlarge my views. Since many of the books listed below have been republished, in some cases numerous times, the dates listed after the title reflect the latest publication date. Brackets indicate the original dates of those considered classics. They are listed by title, rather than author, for easy reference to subjects. I have continued to refer to articles in newspapers and elsewhere right up to the date of publication, and encourage all readers to continue their own education on an ongoing basis so as to be the best advocate for democracy they possibly can be. This work only is a beginning on that quest. The following is a list of books I have used as references to get you started.

*1491*, Charles C. Mann, Vintage, 2011.

*The American Puritans*, Dustin Benge and Nate Pickowicz, Reform Heritage Books, 2020.

*America's Constitution, A Biography*, Akhil Reed Amar, Random House.

*The Awkard Thoughts of W. Kamau Bell,* Dutton, 2017.

*Behave, The Biology of Humans at our Best and Worst,* Robert Sapolsky, Penguin, 2017.

*Biased*, Jennifer L. Eberhardt, Viking, 2019.

*The Bitter and the Sweet: The Saga of a Black Family in America,* Curtis L. Estes, Regent Press, 2021.

*Brighter Climate Futures*, Hari Lamba, Regent Press, 2020.

*Capitalism and Freedom*, Milton Friedman, University of Chicago Press, [1962] 2002.

*China: A History,* John Keay, Basic Books, 2009.

*Collapse: How Societies Choose to Fail or Succeed,* Jared Diamond, Viking, 2005.

*The Collapse of the Third Republic,* William L. Shirer, Simon and Schuster, 1969.

*Common Sense,* Thomas Paine, Penguin, [1776] 2005.

*Constitutions of the World,* Robert L. Maddex, Routledge, 2014.

*Corporations Are Not People,* Jeffery D. Clements, Barrett-Koehler, 2014.

*The Cultural Origins of Human Cognition,* Michael

Tomasello, Harvard University Press, 1999.

*Democracy*, John Dunn, Atlantic Books, 2005.

*Democracy and the Ethical Life: A Philosophy of Politics and Community*, Claes Ryn, Catholic University of America Press, 1990.

*Democracy in America*, Alexis de Tocqueville, Everyman's Library, [1835] 1994.

*Democracy in Chains*, Nancy McLean, Penguin, 2017.

*Disenthralling Ourselves*, Nita Schechet, Farleigh Dickinson University Press, 2009.

*The Emergence of Illiberalism: Understanding a Global Phenomenon*, Edited by Boris Vormann and Michael D. Weinman, Routledge, 2021.

*Energy: Overdevelopment and the Illusion of Endless Growth*, Edited by Tom Butler and George Wuerthner, Post Carbon Institute, 2012.

*Europe: A History*, Norman Davies, Oxford University Press, 1996.

*Europe before Rome*, T. Douglass Price, Oxford University Press, 2012.

*The Fortunes of Africa*, Martin Meredith, Public Affairs, 2014.

*Founding Brothers*, Joseph Ellis, Knopf, 2001.

*France: People, History, and Culture*, Cecil Jenkins, Running Press, 2011.

*Freezing Order*, Bill Browder, Simon and Schuster, 2022.

*The Future of Democracy*, Steve Zolno, Regent Press, 2018.

*The General Theory of Employment, Interest, and Money*, John Maynard Keynes, Harcourt, [1936] 1964.

*Good Economics for Hard Times*, Abhijit Banerjee and Ester Duflo, Public Affairs, 2019.

*The Green Collar Economy: How One Solution Can Fix Our Two Biggest Problems*, Van Jones, HarperCollins, 2008.

*Hall of Mirrors, The Great Depression, the Great Recession, and the Uses – and Misuses – of History*, Barry Eichengreen, Oxford University Press, 2016.

*Hamilton, Adams, Jefferson: The Policies of Enlightenment and The American Founding*, Daren Staloff, Hill and Wang, 2005.

*A History of Egypt*, Jason Thompson, Anchor, 2009.

*How Democracies Die*, Steven Livitsky and Daniel Ziblatt, Crown Publishing, 2018.

*How Rights Went Wrong: Why Our Obsession with Rights Is Tearing America Apart*, Jamal Greene, Houghton Mifflin Harcourt, 2021.

*How We Learn: Why our Brains Learn Better Than any Machine...for Now*, Stanislas Dehaene, Penguin, 2021.

*The Idea of Justice*, Amartya Sen, Harvard University Press, 2009.

*Inequality and Instability*, James Galbraith, Oxford University Press, 2012.

*Jean-Jacques Rousseau: Restless Genius*, Leo Damrosch, Mariner Books, 2007.

*The Jurisprudence of John Marshall*, Robert Kenneth Faulkner, Princeton, 1969.

*The Landmark Thucydides*, Thucydides and Robert B. Strassler, Touchstone, 1998.

*Leviathan*, Thomas Hobbes, Oxford University Press, [1651] 1998.

*Lost Connections, Understanding the Real Causes of Depression – and the Unexpected Solutions*, Johann Hari, Bloomsbury, 2018.

*The Making of a Manager*, Julie Zhou, Portfolio/Penguin, 2019.

*The Man Without a Face: The Unlikely Rise of Vladimir Putin*, Masha Gessen, Riverhead Books, 2012.

*Natural Law and Natural Rights, John Finnis*, Oxford University Press, 2011.

*The Nature of Prejudice*, Gordon W. Allport, Basic Books, 1979.

*On Aggression*, Conrad Lorenz, Harcourt, 1966.

*On Liberty*, John Stuart Mill, Dover, [1859] 2002.

*The Origins of Political Order*, Francis Fukuyama, Farrar, Strauss, and Giroux, 2012.

*The Oxford History of Britain*, Kenneth O. Morgan, Oxford University Press, 2010.

*The Oxford History of the American People,* Samuel Eliot Morison, Oxford University Press, 1965.

*The People vs Democracy*, Yascha Mounk, Harvard University Press, 2018.

*Perfectly Legal*, David Cay Johnston, Portfolio Publishing, 2005.

*The Populist Temptation*, Barry Eichengreen. Oxford University Press, 2018.

*Power and Governance in a Partially Globalized World*, Robert O Keohane, Routledge, 2002.

*The Power of Habit,* Charles Duhigg, Random House, 2014.

*The Price of Inequality*, Joseph Stiglitz, Norton, 2013.

*The Republic, The Complete Works of Plato,* Hacket Press, 1997.

*The Road to Serfdom,* Friedrich Hayek, University of Chicago Press, [1944] 2007.

*Russia: A History*, Gregory L. Freeze, Oxford University Press, 2009.

*Sacred Mountains of the World,* Edwin Bernbaum, Sierra Club, 1990.

*The Social Contract,* John Jacques Rousseau, Penguin, [1762] 1974.

*SPQR*, Mary Beard, Liveright Publishing, 2015.

*The Story of Civilization, Will and Ariel Durant, Simon and Schuster, 1967.*

*Strangers in their Own Land*, Arlie Hochschild, The New Press, 2016.

*The Structure of Scientific Revolutions*, Thomas S. Kuhn, University of Chicago Press, [1962] 2012.

*Team of Rivals*, Doris Kearns Goodwin, Simon and Schuster, 2006.

*A Theory of Justice*, John Rawls, Belknap Press, [1971] 1999.

*Three Days at the Brink*, Brett Baier, William Morrow, 2019.

*A Treatise on Politics*, Bernard Spinoza, Hollyoake and Company, 1854.

*The Triumph of Injustice*, Emmanuel Saez and Gabriel Zucman, Norton, 2019.

*Truth and Democracy*, Steve Zolno, Regent Press, 2020.

*Twilight of Democracy*, Anne Applebaum, Anchor, 2021.

*Unfree Speech: The Threat to Global Democracy and Why We Must Act, Now*, Joshua Wong, Penguin, 2020.

*Walking the Bible*, Bruce Fieler, William Morrow, 2014.

*Water 4.0*, David Sedlak, University of California Press, 2014.

*Why Did Europe Conquer the World?* Philip Hoffman, Princeton University Press, 2017.

*Why We Cooperate*, Michael Tomasello, MIT Press, 2009.

## A Note on Notes

Most books have separate notes for each chapter which, in my experience, makes them difficult to find. That is why, in this book, I use only one set of references which makes them easier to navigate than needing to wade through chapter headings. If a book that is noted lacks a page reference, the reader can assume that the entire book discusses that idea.

# Endnotes

1    "The dogmas of the quiet past are inadequate to the stormy present. The occasion is piled high with difficulty, and we must rise with the occasion. As our case is new, so we must think anew and act anew. We must disenthrall ourselves, and then we shall save our country." Abraham Lincoln, *Annual Message to Congress*, 1862, quoted in *Disenthralling Ourselves*, Page 13.

2    "...government of the people, by the people, for the people, shall not perish from the earth." *Lincoln's Gettysburg Address*, 1863.

3    "For bands and tribes, social organization is based on kinship, and these societies are relatively egalitarian." *The Origins of Political Order*, Page 53.

4    "Everywhere that the word *democracy* has fought its way forward across time and space, you can hear both these themes: the purposeful struggle to improve the practical circumstances of life and to escape from arbitrary and often brutal coercion, but also the determination and longing to be treated with respect and some degree of consideration." *Democracy*, Page 19.

5    "Categorization can impede our efforts to embrace and understand people who are deemed not like us, by tuning us to the faces of people who look like us and dampening our sensitivity to those who don't." *Biased*, Page 24.

6    "As we lose the ability to listen to each other, democracy becomes less meaningful and closer to the consensus of various tribes, who each vote based more on tribal loyalties than on a judicious balancing of priorities." *Good Economics for Hard Times*, Page 135.

7  "Washington D.C. felt very far away...everyone I talked to ...felt like victims of a frightening loss – or was it theft? – of their cultural home, their place in the world, and their honor." *Strangers in their Own Land*, Page 48.

8  Genesis 2:10–24. *New Oxford Annotated Bible*, 1973.

9  "Whatever form the modern national constitution takes, its primary goal should be to define the limitations on those who rule at the highest level in a nation-state." *Constitutions of the World*, Page viii.

10  "We must forever conduct our struggle on the high plane of dignity and discipline. We must not allow our creative protest to degenerate into physical violence. Again and again, we must rise to the majestic heights of meeting physical force with soul force." *I Have a Dream Speech*, August 28, 1963.

11  "Hatred...is most dangerous. It [is an] exchange [of] one slavery for another. We must get rid of this feeling. Our quarrel is not with the British people, we fight their imperialism." *Gandhi's "Quit India" Speech*, August 8, 1942.

12  "I have fought against white domination and I have fought against black domination. I have carried the ideal of a democratic and free society in which all persons live together in harmony and with equal opportunity. It is an ideal which I hope to live for and to achieve. But, if needs be, it is an ideal for which I am prepared to die." Mandela's 1964 speech, with the exact same words repeated in 1990.

13  "To an unprecedented degree, homo sapiens are adapted for acting and thinking cooperatively in cultural groups, and indeed all of humans' most impressive cognitive achievements – from complex technologies to linguistic and mathematical symbols to intricate social

institutions – are the products not of individuals acting alone, but of individuals interacting." *Why We Cooperate*, Page XV.

14 "Lack of social contact, and above all deprivation of it, were among the factors strongly predisposing to facilitate aggression." *On Aggression*, Page 50.

15 *Europe before Rome*, Page 55.

16 *Democracy*, Page 32.

17 Example of dialogue between Socrates and his student Thrasymachus from *Plato's Republic*:

S: "Are the rulers in all cities infallible, or are they liable to error?" T: "No doubt they are liable to error." S: "When they undertake to make laws, therefore, they make some correctly, others incorrectly?" T: "I suppose so." S: "And a law is correct if it prescribes what is to the rulers' own advantage and incorrect if it prescribes what is to their disadvantage?" T: "It is." S: "And whatever laws they make must be obeyed by their subjects, and this is justice?" T: "Of course." S: "Then, according to your own account, it is just to do not only what is to the advantage of the stronger, but also the opposite, what is not to their advantage." *The Republic, The Complete Works of Plato*, 339c (section number from the Greek manuscript).

18 *The Landmark Thucydides*, Page 112.

19 *SPQR*, Page 97.

20 *SPQR*, Pages 21 and 218.

21 *Europe: A History*, Page 412.

22 *Europe: A History*, Page 479.

23 *The Oxford History of the American People*, Page 483.

24 *The Oxford History of the American People*, Page 762.

25 *Child Labor in the United States,* History.com Editors, April 17, 2020.

26 "God gave [Adam] not private dominion over the inferior creatures, but right in common with all mankind." *First Treatise of Government*, John Locke, Cambridge University Press, [1703] 1992, Page 157.

27 Rousseau influenced the American Founders. He is not mentioned in their writings, but there are clear similarities between parts of *The Social Contract* and The Declaration of Independence. Here are three sources who present the view that Rousseau had a direct influence:

"The first sign of [Rousseau's] political influence was in the wave of public sympathy that supported active French aid to the American Revolution. Jefferson derived the Declaration of Independence from Rousseau as well as from Locke and Montesquieu. As ambassador to France (1785–89) he absorbed much from both Voltaire and Rousseau...The success of the American Revolution raised the prestige of Rousseau's pilosophy." *The Story of Civilization,* Will and Ariel Durant, 1967, Simon and Schuster, Pages 890-91.

"In a series of amazingly original books, of which The Social Contract is best known, [Rousseau] developed a political theory that deeply influenced the American Founding Fathers and the French revolutionaries." *Jean-Jacques Rousseau: Restless Genius*, Leo Damrosch, Mariner Books, 2007, Page 1.

"Knowingly or unknowingly echoing Rousseau, he (Jefferson) describes it as a pleasurable feeling of benevolence towards others which 'prompts us irresistibly to feel and succor their distresses." *Democracy and the Ethical Life: A Philosophy of Politics and Community,* Claes Ryn, Catholic University of America Press, 1990, Page 186.

28 "Montesquieu believes that the laws of many countries can be made be more liberal and more humane, and that they can often be applied less arbitrarily, with less scope for the unpredictable and oppressive use of state power. Likewise, religious persecution and slavery can be abolished, and commerce can be encouraged. These reforms would generally strengthen monarchical governments, since they enhance the freedom and dignity of citizens." *Stanford Encyclopedia of Philosophy*.

29 *On Liberty*, Page 4.

30 Direct influences on Jefferson were *Essays on the Principles of Morality and Natural Religion* by Lord Kames, Henry Home, of which Jefferson had a personal copy, "advocated that men had an inner sense of right and wrong," and *Discourses Concerning Government*, by Algernon Sidney, "probably the best elementary book of the principles of government," according to Jefferson. From *Thomas Jefferson, Declaration of Independence: Right to Institute New Government*, US Library of Congress.

31 *Democracy in America*, Page 263.

32 "Given the right conditions, any society can turn against democracy...The (US) electoral college was originally meant to be...a kind of review board, a group of elite lawmakers and men of property who would select the president, rejecting the people's choice if necessary, in order to avoid the 'excesses of democracy (Hamilton).' " *Twilight of Democracy*, Page 14.

33 *Gettysburg Address*. "If a kingdom is divided against itself, that kingdom cannot stand. And if a house is divided against itself, that house will not be able to stand." This is a paraphrase of Mark 3:24-25, *New Oxford Annotated Bible*, 1973.

34 "Over time political democracies create an environment within which 'economic democracy'

can arise in the form of powerful trade unions, social democratic parties, responsive legislatures, and other equalizing institutions." *Inequality and Instability*, Page 103.

35 "Illiberal forces quickly seek to fill the ideological vacuum left by a hollowed out liberal idealism. Once in office, however, demagogues not only fail to deliver most of their promises, but also and perhaps most importantly, later the structure of the state and civil society in ways that are likely to inflict long term damage." *The Emergence of Illiberalism: Understanding a Global Phenomenon*, Page 4.

36 "The year 1991...marked the dissolution of the USSR into fifteen sovereign republics, the largest of which was the Russian Federation." *Russia: A History*, Page 462.

37 "By the summer of 1957 all those who had been rash enough to speak out were rounded up....Alleviating the conditions meant admitting the disaster, but since the leadership and its policies were beyond criticism, those responsible must be incompetent or reactionary elements within the communes.....How many victims were claimed by the famine of 1958-61 will never be known. It was certainly the century's worst... statisticians have extrapolated a catch-all figure of 20-30 million. *China: A History*, Pages 523-25.

38 *Europe must stop this disgrace: Viktor Orbán is dismantling democracy*, Timothy Garton Ash, The Guardian, June 20, 2019.

39 *The Bitter and the Sweet*, Pages 107-08.

40 "The Republican legislature and governor have made a breathtaking assertion of partisan power in elections, making absentee voting harder and creating restrictions and complications." *What Georgia's Voting*

*Law Really Does,* Nick Corasaniti and Reid J. Epstein, April 2, 2021, NY Times.

41 *Election officials in Texas reject hundreds of ballot applications under state's new voting restrictions,* Eugene Scott, Washington Post, January 15, 2022.

42 *America's Constitution, A Biography,* Page 126.

43 This was part of Hammurabi's code from Mesopotamia in the 18th century BCE: "If a man has destroyed the eye of a man of the gentleman class, they shall destroy his eye."

44 "There is a substantial body of literature about how different parts of the brain often are in conflict about whether to act rationally or emotionally." *Behave, The Biology of Humans at our Best and Worst,* Pages 27-30.

45 Thomas Hobbes tells us that without "Commonwealth," or government, there is perpetual strife between people and we cannot experience peace. *Leviathan,* Page 164.

46 *The People vs Democracy,* Page 9.

47 *Estonia Turns the Page on its Flirtation with the Right-wing EKRE,* Andrew MacDowell, World Politics Review, October 29, 2021.

48 *Twilight of Democracy,* Page 14.

49 "By a faction, I understand a number of citizens, whether amounting to a majority or a minority of the whole, who are united and actuated by some common impulse of passion, or of interest, adverse to the rights of other citizens, or to the permanent and aggregate interests of the community." James Madison, *Federalist #10,* 1787.

50 *Founding Brothers,* Page 235.

51  *Outcry as memorial to Tiananmen Square victims removed from Hong Kong University,* Rhoda Kwan and Vincent Ni, The Guardian, December 23, 2021.

52  *Trump's Next Coup Has Already Begun,* Barton Gellman, The Atlantic, December 6, 2021.

53  "In 2015, the [European] Commission launched an investigation...of Polish legislation...that compromised the independence of the...country's supreme court, and that subjected Poland's public broadcasters to state control...at roughly the same time, the commission launched an infringement case against the Hungarian government...for a restrictive refugee law that conflicted with the Common European Asylum System and for erecting a steel fence along the country's southern border." *The Populist Temptation*, Page 143.

54  *Washington Post contributor arrested in Moscow after criticizing Putin,* Paul Farhi and Roby Dixon, Washington Post, April 12, 2022.

55  Vladimir Putin, talking on TV about what he claimed were Chechnyan terrorists: "We will hunt them down... Wherever we find them we will destroy them." *The Man Without a Face: The Unlikely Rise of Vladimir Putin*, Page 26.

56  *Constitutions of the World,* 2014.

57  "There is a body of literature in political science arguing that democracies tend to be egalitarian, as compared to authoritarian or dictatorial regimes....we find the result holds only for a subclass of democracy, namely social democracies that have been in stable existence for a long period of time." *Inequality and Instability*, Page 15.

58  *Putin's war propaganda becomes 'patriotic' lessons in Russian schools,* Mary Ilyushina, Washington Post, March 20, 2022.

59  James Madison had concerns about the viability of democracy that he expressed in *The Federalist,* Number 55.

60  *Hamilton, Adams, Jefferson: The Policies of Enlightenment and The American Founding,* Page 8.

61  The Montgomery Bus Boycott of 1955, The Grape Boycott of 1965-70, and international sanctions of South Africa to defeat Apartheid all took an economic toll on those perpetuating injustices.

62  ""Virtually every state government, according to a recent study by the nonpartisan Center for Public Integrity, kowtows to business and the wealthy, underrepresents citizens of lesser means, lacks transparency, and does a poor job of enforcing ethics laws." *Democracy in Chains,* Page 230.

63  "To end loneliness, you need other people – plus something else. You also need...to feel you are sharing something with the other person, or the group, that is meaningful to both of you." *Lost Connections, Understanding the Real Causes of Depression – and the Unexpected Solutions,* Page 100.

64  "In less than half a year, the Soviet Union would effectively collapse, and Yeltsin would become the leader of a new, democratic Russia. That this was inevitable had become clear to many people, including me, that March day, when the people of Russia had defied the Communist government and it tanks and insisted on having their way in the public square." *The Man Without a Face: The Unlikely Rise of Vladimir Putin,* Page 5.

65  See the very first footnote, above.

66  *The Origins of Political Order,* Pages 70-71.

67  *Walking the Bible,* Page 174.

68  Exodus 20:1-17, *New Oxford Annotated Bible*.

69  *Natural Law and Natural Rights, John Finnis*, Page 83.

70  *Democracy*, Page 26.

71  *America's Constitution: A Biography*, Page 20.

72  "Since all men, whether barbarous or civilized, everywhere must submit themselves to the yoke of customs, and form a kind of social existence, the customs and foundations of government must not be sought in the formulas of reason, but must be deduced from the common nature or condition of men." *A Treatise on Politics*, Page 15.

73  *A Theory of Justice*, Page 11.

74  *The Idea of Justice*, Pages xiii and 155.

75  *Hong Kong police make first arrests under new security law, Ben Soo*, Associated Press, June 30, 2020.

76  *France: People, History, and Culture*, Page 110.

77  *The Collapse of the Third Republic*.

78  *GOP lawmakers push historic wave of bills targeting rights of LGBTQ teens, children and their families*, Kimberly Kindy, Washington Post, March 25, 2022.

79  *Justice Dept to Expand Training Offered to Local Law Enforcement*, Katie Benner, New York Times, March 18, 2022.

80  *Biased*, Page 24.

81  *Behave, The Biology of Humans at our Best and Worst*, Page 45.

82  *The Structure of Scientific Revolutions*, Page 66.

83  "To learn, our brain must first form a hypothetical mental model of the outside world, which it then projects

onto its environment and puts to a test by comparing its predictions to what it received from the senses." *How We Learn: Why our Brains Learn Better Than any Machine... For Now*, Page 178.

84 *The Nature of Prejudice*, Pages 39-40.

85 "The idea of continental drift, for example, took sixty years to become accepted." *Continental Drift: The groundbreaking theory of moving continents,* Becky Oskin, Live Science Newsletter, December 14, 2021.

86 "Over time, the instinctive defensive reaction we started from is replaced by a carefully constructed set of seemingly robust arguments. At that point, we start feeling that any disagreement with our views, given how solid the 'arguments' are, has to be either an insinuation of moral failure on our part or questioning our intelligence." *Good Economics for Hard Times*, Page 120.

87 *The Nature of Prejudice*, Page 449.

88 This became clear when I interviewed teachers during my visit there in 2015.

89 *Book Ban Efforts Spread Across the U.S,* Elizabeth A. Harris and Alexandra Alter, New York Times, January 30, 2021; *The Epidemic of Book Bannings Must Be Read as a Warning,* **Amy Goodman & Denis Moynihan,** Democracy Now, February 3, 2022.

90 "Project-based learning is a dynamic classroom approach in which students actively explore real-world problems and challenges and acquire a deeper knowledge." *Project-Based Learning (PBL),* Edutopia Website.

91 "In the Soviet Union the first Five-Year Plan (1928–32), implemented by Joseph Stalin, concentrated on developing heavy industry and collectivizing agriculture, at the cost of a drastic fall in consumer goods. The second

Five-Year Plan (1933–37) continued the objectives of the first. Collectivization, coupled with other Stalinist policies, led to terrible famines that caused the deaths of millions of people." *Five-Year Plans,* The Editors of Encyclopedia Britannica, Mar 28, 2022.

92 *Donald Trump praises strong Vladimir Putin amid outrage over defense of Russia,* David Mercer, Sky News, July 18, 2018.

93 *Democracy in Chains,* Pages 139.

94 *Truckers and protesters against Covid-19 mandates block a border crossing,* Paula Newton and Holly Yan, CNN, February 1, 2022.

95 *Hong Kong's immunized who died of COVID mainly got Sinovac vaccine,* Bloomberg, March 20, 2022.

96 *Energy: Overdevelopment and the Illusion of Endless Growth,* Page 225.

97 "Amid a public health crisis, sycophantic TV hosts are glorifying the president and attacking his perceived enemies, treating a pandemic like yet another partisan fight." *Fox Goes Full Dear Leader With Coronavirus Coverage,* Caleb Ecarma, Vanity Fair, March 11, 2020.

98 "There is widespread suppression of politically sensitive material in much of the media. Journalists who criticise the authorities face possible reprisals, including physical violence and judicial harassment. Critical media outlets are subject to various pressures, including economic pressure, making it difficult for them to remain commercially viable. The number and reach of independent media have greatly diminished during Vladimir Putin's years in power." *Russia profile – Media,* BBC News, 8 June 2021.

99 Genesis 3:19. *New Oxford Annotated Bible.*

100 "In the Ohlone, world religion was not isolated from daily life...Everything was religious." *The Ohlone Way*, Page 143.

101 *Europe before Rome*, 2013.

102 "For many of us, [mountains are] a place of spiritual renewal, where we can go back to the source of our being and recover the freshness of a new beginning." *Sacred Mountains of the World*, Page 252.

103 "75% of Americans now believe humans fuel climate change. Two recent polls underscore Americans' shifting attitudes on climate change." Stephen Johnson, *Think Big*, September 16, 2019.

104 *Energy: Overdevelopment and the Illusion of Endless Growth*, Page 225.

105 *UN Report Warns Climate Crisis is Driving Hunger, Poverty, Disease and Species Loss*, Democracy Now, February 28, 2022.

106 *Collapse: How Societies Choose to Fail or Succeed*, Pages 427-430.

107 "Climate change can impact air quality and, conversely, air quality can impact climate change." Air Quality and Climate Change Research, US Environmental Protection Agency Website.

108 *Brighter Climate Futures*, Pages 101 and 144.

109 *Climate Change Raises Risk of Major Wildfires*, Raymond Zhong, New York Times, February 23, 2022.

110 *Water 4.0*, David Sedlak, Page 192.

111 *The Trouble with America's Water*, Lynne Peoples, The Guardian, September 25, 2020.

112 *Plastic pollution is exploding while policies to address the problem remain weak*, Shirin Ali, The Hill, February 22, 2022.

113  *The FDA found 'forever chemicals' in meat, seafood, and chocolate cake found in grocery stores. Here's how worried you should be,* Aria Bendix, Business Insider, June 4, 2019.

114  "Low-lying south Florida, at the front line of climate change in the US, will be swallowed as sea levels rise. Astonishingly, the population is growing, house prices are rising and building goes on. The problem is the city is run by climate change deniers." *Miami, the great world city, is drowning while the powers that be look away*, Robin McKie, The Guardian, Friday 11 July 2014.

115  *Overfishing – the Most Serious Threat to our Oceans,* Environmental Defense Fund.

116  *Death in the forest,* Terrence McCoy, Washington Post, March 17, 2022.

117  "A federal judge this week required the government to take climate change into account before approving offshore oil drilling leases. That's becoming more common." *Judges Increasingly Demand Climate Analysis in Drilling Decisions.* Lisa Friedman, *New York Times,* Jan. 28, 2022.

118  *Federal Judge Cancels Biden Administration's Largest-Ever Offshore Drilling Lease Sale*, Democracy Now, Jan 28, 2022.

119  "Carbon capture, utilization and storage (CCUS), also referred to as carbon capture, utilization and sequestration, is a process that captures carbon dioxide emissions from sources like coal-fired power plants and either reuses or stores it so it will not enter the atmosphere." US Department of Energy Website.

120  "Carlsberg and Coca-Cola back pioneering project to make 'all-plant' drink bottles." *The end of plastic? New plant-based bottles will degrade in a year*. Jillian Ambrose, The Guardian, May 16, 2020.

121 "Representatives of 175 nations have reached a historic agreement to reduce pollution from plastic. Negotiators at the United Nations Environment Assembly in Kenya agreed Wednesday to draft a new global treaty that could ban single-use plastic, while promoting the sustainable design of products and the reuse of materials. A recent U.N. study found that unless nations limit waste, the weight of plastic pollution in the world's oceans could exceed the weight of all the world's fish within two decades."*175 Countries Agree to Collectively Tackle Plastic Pollution Crisis*, Democracy Now, Mar 03, 2022.

122 "2022 is set to be a record year in terms of the scale at which the switchover from fossil fuels to renewable sources will take place." *The Five Biggest New Energy Trends In 2022*, Bernard Marr, Forbes, March 1, 2022.

123 *United Airlines just became the first airline in history to operate a passenger flight using 100% sustainable aviation fuel. Taylor Rains, Business Insider, Dec 1, 2021.*

124 *Investors turn up the heat on companies over climate change.* Charles Riley, CNN Business, September 18, 2019.

125 *JPMorgan Chase Will Halt Financing of Arctic Oil, Gas Drilling, Coal Plants.* Garet Bleir, February 25, 2020, Sierra Club Magazine.

126 *Electric Vehicles Take Center Stage at 2022 Chicago Auto Show,* February 17, 2022, Kane Farabaugh, VOA.

127 *Court Orders EPA to Ban Chlorpyrifos, Pesticide Tied to Children's Health Problems*, Eric Lipton, New York Times, August 9, 2018.

128 "The use of renewable energy is influenced by Finland's own energy and climate policies, the

obligations and policy decisions under European Union climate and energy legislation, which have the EU committed to achieving climate neutrality by 2050." *Finland – Country Commercial Guide, International Trade Administration*, 09-14-21.

129  "Here's how a formidable clean energy coalition helped pass the most equitable climate legislation in the country—and developed a blueprint for other states to follow." *Illinois Shows Us What the Road to Clean Energy Should Look Like.* Courtney Lindwall, National Resource Defense Council, December 02, 2021.

130  "The task at hand is not just to win equal protection from the worst of global warming and the other negative effects that go hand in hand with ecological disaster. It also is to win equal opportunity and equal access to the bounty of the green economy, with its manifold positive opportunities." *Green Collar Economy: How One Solution Can Fix Our Two Biggest Problems,* Page 71.

131  "Behind a rising number of outages are new stresses on the system caused by aging power lines, a changing climate and a power-plant fleet is rapidly going green." *America's Power Grid Is Increasingly Unreliable,* Katherine Blunt, Wall Street Journal, Feb. 18, 2022.

132  *Energy: Overdevelopment and the Illusion of Endless Growth,* Page 17.

133  *10 steps you can take to lower your carbon footprint,* Washington Post Staff, February 22, 2022.

134  *Brighter Climate Futures,* Pages 101 and 144.

135  *The Structure of Scientific Revolutions,* Page 6.

136  *Democracy,* Page 35.

137  *Europe: A History,* Page 130.

138  *SPQR,* Pages 125-28.

139   *Europe: A History,* Page 131.

140   *The Oxford History of Britain,* Page 150.

141   *The Oxford History of the American People,* Pages 49-53.

142   *The American Puritans,* Pages 17-20.

143   *America's Constitution: A Biography,* Pages 5-7.

144   "After ordainment, Americans from consenting states would indeed 'form a more perfect union' that prohibited unilateral exit." *America's Constitution: A Biography,* Page 21.

145   *America's Constitution: A Biography,* Page 151.

146   In "all very numerous assemblies, of whatever character composed, passion never fails to wrest the scepter from reason." *The Federalist,* Number 55.

147   *Who Voted in Early America?,* Constitutional Rights Foundation Website.

148   *"We say gay!" Florida Students Walk Out to Protest Anti-LGBTQ+ Legislation,* Democracy Now, March 8, 2022.

149   *Election officials in Texas reject hundreds of ballot applications under state's new voting restrictions,* Eugene Scott, Washington Post, January 15, 2022.

150   "Ten state chief election officials say in interviews they have had to refocus their positions to battle a constant flow of disinformation. This year, they say, will be no different." *Election officials are on the frontlines of defending democracy. They didn't sign up for this.* Zach Montellaro, Politico, February 16, 2022.

151   *The Tunisian President's Election Plan Is Troubling. So Is the U.S. Response.* Carnegie Endowment for International Peace, Sarah Yerkes, December 21, 2021.

152   *U.S. Sanctions Nicaraguan Gov't as President Ortega Sidelines Opponents Ahead of Election,* Democracy Now, November 05, 2021.

153   *With US Afghanistan Exit, Russia's Power in Central Asia Grows Ever Stronger,* New York Times, August 20, 2021.

154   "Each person is to have an equal right to the most extensive basic liberty compatible with similar liberty for others." *A Theory of Justice,* Page 53.

155   "The problem is to find a form of association which will defend and protect with the whole commonforce the person and goals of each associate, and in which each, while uniting himself with all, may still obey himself alone and remain as free as before." Jean Jacques Rousseau, *The Social Contract,* Pages 3 and 10.

156   "Deep-seated animosity around abortion policies is not universal. It is relatively absent, for example, in Canada or in much of Europe and Asia. Among the many reasons for this difference, American courts' insistence on choosing between rights....[In Roe v. Wade, 1973] The opinion's insistence that a fetus was not a constitutional person pushed the [anti-abortion] movement into a more radical, disruptive posture. Hardliners pursued a 'human life amendment' to the Constitution that would define a fetus as entitled to constitutional rights from the moment of conception, with no exception even for an abortion necessary to save the life of a pregnant woman." *How Rights Went Wrong: Why Our Obsession with Rights Is Tearing America Apart,* Pages 115 and 120.

157   *The Landmark Thucydides,* Pages 520-21.

158   *SPQR,* Mary Beard, Page 218.

159   "He was a populist hero and a corrupt demagogue, hailed as a champion of the poor and reviled as a dictator.

Louisiana's Huey Long built his remarkable career as governor and U.S. Senator on a platform of social reform and justice, all the while employing graft and corruption to get what he wanted." Publicity about the film *Huey Long* by Ken Burns, 1986.

160 *China claims its authoritarian one-party system is a democracy -- and one that works better than the US,* Nectar Gan and Steve George, CNN, December 8, 2021.

161 *A brief history of Donald Trump's mixed messages on freedom of speech,* Jenna Johnson, Washington Post, September 29, 2017.

162 Among the worst examples in history are the "great purges" of Stalin. "The trials successfully eliminated the major real and potential political rivals and critics of Joseph Stalin. The trials were the public aspect of the widespread purge that sent millions of alleged 'enemies of the people' to prison camps in the 1930s. **Great Purge,** Soviet history, The Editors of Encyclopedia Britannica, March 6, 2022.

163 "The people have an original right to establish... principles...most conducive to their own happiness. [This is] fundamental and...permanent." John Marshall in *Marbury v Madison*, 1803. Quoted in *The Jurisprudence of John Marshall,* Page 198.

164 "Today, an approach called 'proportionality' though exotic in the United States, dominates courts around the world. A structured way of setting rights against government interests, proportionality would have resonated with America's founders but today is more commonly associated with Canadians and Germans. Courts that adopt proportionality tend to recognize a wide range of rights – far wider than in the United States – but the court's attention trains on the ways in which government can, or can't, limit those rights. In these

other countries, limiting rights is not just something the government can do in an emergency when the time bomb is ticking. Rather rights are *inherently* limited." *How Rights Went Wrong: Why Our Obsession with Rights is Tearing America Apart,* Jamal Greene, Houghton Mifflin Harcourt, 2012. Pages xxii-xxiii.

165 "Most people actually want to work, not just because they need the money; work brings with it a sense of purpose, belonging, dignity." *Good Economics for Hard Times,* Page 299.

166 "Personal responsibility is a deeply resonant value that promises to empower the 'lowly' and to reconcile us to our political world. As such, it can play an important role in revitalizing our impoverished political and institutional imagination." *Responsibility Redefined,* Yascha Mounk, Democracy Journal, Winter, 2017.

167 *Donald Trump praises 'strong' Vladimir Putin amid outrage over defense of Russia,* David Mercer, Sky News, July 18, 2018.

168 *Three Days at the Brink,* Page 160.

169 *America Could Have Done So Much More to Protect Ukraine,* Alexander Vindman, The Atlantic, February 24, 2022.

170 "As the U.S.-funded broadcaster is forced to shut most of its Russian operations, its Web traffic indicates that Russian people are eagerly consuming its stories," *The Kremlin tries to stifle Radio Free Europe — and its audience surges,* Margaret Sullivan, Washington Post, March 27, 2022.

171 *China, Democracy that Works.* China's State Council on Information Office, December 4, 2021.

172 "In supporting Hong Kong in its resistance against the Communist regime, the international community

is contributing to a broader fight against the spread of tyranny that, like climate change and terrorism, threatens the way of life and liberty everywhere." *Unfree Speech: The Threat to Global Democracy and Why We Must Act, Now,* Page 247.

173   *Freezing Order,* Bill Browder, Simon and Schuster, 2022, Pages 28-30.

174   *As Putin eyes Ukraine invasion, Trump praises his actions as "genius,"* Olivia Rubin, *ABC News*, February 23, 2022.

175   *U.S. less effective at countering terrorist threats in Afghanistan and Somalia since troop withdrawal, generals warn,* Karoun Demirjian, Washington Post, March 15, 2022.

176   *Europe: A History*, Page 76.

177   *A History of Egypt,* Pages 13-26.

178   *1491*, Page 136.

179   *The Fortunes of Africa*, Page 26.

180   *Inequality and Instability*, Page 3.

181   Sometimes it works better for all involved to loan money to debtors to allow them to continue paying their debts. *Greek Debt Crisis Explained,* Kimberly Amadeo, The Balance, May 17, 2020.

182   "The dominant narrative of the Great Depression, that it was caused by avoidable policy failures, was conducive to the belief that those failures could be – and had been – corrected....To the contrary, the long period of economic stability...encouraged investors to take on additional risk." *Hall of Mirrors, The Great Depression, the Great Recession, and the Uses – and Misuses – of History,* Page 379.

183   "Democratic principles require that some level of

participation in making collective decisions be open to all competent adults in the society." *Power and Governance in a Partially Globalized World*, Page 250.

184   *Perfectly Legal*, Pages 209-18.

185   "The (2008) financial crisis...was the consequence of a deliberate effort to sustain a model of economic growth based on inequality...By pressing this model past all legal and ethical limits, the US succeeded in... ensuring that when the collapse came, it would utterly destroy the financial sector." *Inequality and Instability*, Page 293.

186   "The share of US national income earned by the 1% has increased from 10% in 1980 to about 20% today...the wealthy save a higher percent of their income than the rest of the population, which allows them to accumulate more wealth, which in turn generates more income." *The Triumph of Injustice*, Page xv.

187   *Wall Street Money Behind New Bill To Repeal Dodd-Frank Act Reforms*, Lydia O'Neal, People' Action Website, May 5, 2017.

188   "The central choice is not between the "free market" and government; it is between a marker organized for broadly based prosperity and one designed to deliver almost all the gains to a few at the top." *Saving Capitalism*, Robert Reich, Page 219.

189   "The most conservative economics department in the world." *Democracy in Chains*, Page 35.

190   "What our planners demand is a central direction of all economic activity according to a single plan, laying down how the resources of society should be 'consciously directed' to serve particular ends in a definite way." *The Road to Serfdom*, Page 85.

191   "To prohibit the use of certain poisonous

substances or require special precautions in their use, to limit working hours or to require certain sanitary arrangements, is fully compatible with the preservation of competition." *The Road to Serfdom*, Page 86.

192 "Fundamentally, there are only two ways of coordinating the economic activity of millions. One is central direction involving the use of coercion – the technique of the army and the modern totalitarian state. The other is voluntary cooperation of individuals – the technique of the market place." *Capitalism and Freedom*, Page 13.

193 "The Glass-Steagall Act's primary objectives were twofold – to stop the unprecedented run on banks and restore public confidence in the U.S. banking system; and to sever the linkages between commercial and investment banking that were believed to have been responsible for the 1929 market crash." *What was the 'Glass-Steagall Act?* Investopedia Website.

194 "The State will have to exercise a guiding influence on the propensity to consume partly through its scheme of taxation, partly by fixing the rate of interest, and partly, perhaps in other ways....It is not the ownership of the instruments of production which is important for the State to assume." *General Theory of Employment, Interest, and Money, John Maynard Keynes,* Page 378.

195 *Boris Johnson's biggest lie about Europe is finally coming home to roost,* Simon Jenkins, The Guardian, September 6, 2021.

196 "Connected institutions funded by the Koch Brothers...included the Cato Institute, the Heritage Foundation, Americans for Prosperity, Freedom Works, the Club for Growth, the State Policy Network, The Competitive Enterprise Institute, the Tax Foundation, the Reason Foundation, the Leadership Foundation, and

more." *Democracy in Chains,* Page xxi.

197  "The new owner has altered the political stance of 'one of the world's great newspapers,' " *The Sunday Times under Murdoch,* Denis Herbstein, Sage Publishing Index on Censorship, April, 1984.

198  *Gradually, Theatrically, Kremlim Puts in Place its Rationale for Invasion,* Anton Troianovksi, New York Times, February 23, 2022.

199  "In 2010...the Supreme Court proclaimed that the American people are not permitted to determine how much control corporations and concentrated wealth may have over elections and lawmakers...a 5-4 decision ruled that federal election law designed to prevent corporations and unions from dominating elections and government violated First Amendment free speech rights. The impact of the Supreme Court folly now is beyond dispute. More money was spent by fewer donors in the 2012 election ever before in history." *Corporations Are Not People,* Page 8.

200  "Recognition is not a good that can be consumed. Rather, it is an intersubjective state of mind by which one being acknowledges the worth or status of another human being." *The Origins of Political Order,* Page 41.

201  "Materialistic people, who think happiness comes from accumulating stuff and a superior status, had much higher levels of depression and anxiety." *Lost Connections, Understanding the Real Causes of Depression – and the Unexpected Solutions,* Page 114.

202  *The Price of Inequality,* Page 30.

203  *Russians Must Accept the Truth. We Failed.,* Ilia Krasilshchik, New York Times, March 16, 2022. Mr. Krasilshchik is the former publisher of Meduza, an independent news outlet.

204  "In Russia, the town that later became Moscow was settled in 1146. Novgorod, an independent municipality in the far north that was ruled by an assembly of free citizens, lasted for centuries. It extended its influence in many directions and repulsed a number of invasions, including one by Sweden in 1240, under the leadership of the legendary Alexander Nevsky. It eventually lost its wars – and independence – to Moscow in 1478, when Ivan III slaughtered its population." *Europe: A History,* Page 386.

205  *How a Five-Day War With Georgia Allowed Russia to Reassert Its Military Might,* Sarah Pruitt, History Channel, Sep 4, 2018.

206  *Syrians recount horror under Russian air attacks,* Shawn Yuan, Al Jazeera, March 5, 2022.

207  "Churchill wrote that Britain had a choice 'between shame and war': 'we have chosen shame and we will get war.' " *Europe: A History,* Page 990.

208  "In the spring of 1938 [Hitler] began to make noises about the intolerable oppression of Germans in the Sudetenland of Czechoslovakia....Democratic governments who neglect the moral fundamentals negotiate with dictators at their peril." *Europe: A History,* Page 987.

209  *Human rights and democracy eroding worldwide,* US finds, Missy Ruan, Washington Post, April 12, 2022.

210  International tribunals were established under the United Nations after World War II to prosecute war criminals.

211  *U.S. less effective at countering terrorist threats in Afghanistan and Somalia since troop withdrawal, generals warn,* Karoun Demirjian, Washington Post, March 15, 2022.

212 *Afghan Officials Estimate More Than 13,000 Infants Have Died of Hunger Since January,* Democracy Now, March 22, 2022.

213 *Nearly 20 years of war, 10 days to fall: Afghanistan, by the numbers,* Adela Suliman, Washington Post, August 20, 2021.

214 *Just How Frightening Is France's New Right?* Thomas Chatterton Williams, The Atlantic, December 9, 2021.

215 *G.O.P. Declares Jan. 6 Attack 'Legitimate Political Discourse,'* Jonathan Weisman and Reid J. Epstein, New York Times, Feb. 4, 2022.

216 *How Democracies Die,* Page 3.

217 *Why Did Europe Conquer the World?* Philip Hoffman, Page 2.

218 *The Power of Habit,* Pages 92-93.

219 "The desire for recognition ensures that politics will never be reducible to simple economic self-interest. Human beings make constant judgments about the intrinsic value, worth, or dignity of other people or institutions, and they organize themselves into hierarchies based on those valuations." *The Origins of Political Order,* Page 45.

220 W. Kamau Bell, a Black American humorist, has interviewed members of the Ku Klux Klan on television in a respectful manner that convinced them to open up and discuss their views on camera. *The Awkard Thoughts of W. Kamau Bell,* Page 4.

221 A partial list of examples of state policies based on considering some populations less than fully human includes the near elimination of Native American tribes by Europeans, slavery of blacks by Southern planters, genocide by Turkey against Armenians, the campaign

to eliminate Tibetans and Uyghurs by China, plans to eliminate Jews by Nazi Germany, the extermination of "enemies of the state" by Stalin, genocide against the Rohingya in Burma, use of poisonous gas against his own people by Bashar al-Assad of Syrian, attacks on people of the Tigray region by Ethiopia, bombing of civilians in Yemen by Saudi Arabia, and the confiscation of Palestinian lands by Israel.

222   During my visit to Russia in 2015, our guide insisted that Chechnya – a region that claims independence – "belongs to us." The idea that people can belong to others shows the effectiveness of propaganda in a country where autocracy dominates the media.

223   *Decline in Immigration Threatens Growth of Regions on the Rise*, Miriam Jordan, New York Times, August 10, 2021.

224   *The Making of a Manager*, Page 83.

225   *It took a war for Big Tech to take a side,* Peter Kafka, Vox, March 9, 2022.

226      https://freedomhouse.org/countries/freedom-world/scores?sort=desc&order=Total%20Score%20and%20Status

227   For an example, Freedom House releases an annual report on which countries have advanced in the realm of democracy and which have regressed. *Freedom in the World 2021, Democracy under Siege,* by Freedom House.

228   "More than $1.5 billion has been spent to settle claims of police misconduct involving thousands of officers repeatedly accused of wrongdoing. Taxpayers are often in the dark." *The hidden billion-dollar cost of repeated police misconduct,* Keith L. Alexander, Steven Rich, and Hannah Thacker, Washington Post, March 9, 2022.

229   *Block the Vote: How Politicians are Trying to Block*

*Voters from the Ballot Box,* American Civil Liberties Union, August 18, 2021.

230   "The Fox News host suddenly decided to backpedal on Thursday night, after he was extensively quoted on Russia's state-run TV...if you missed Carlson's most recent shows, a quick recap of commentary he's offered on the situation: It's "not un-American" to support Putin; Democrats will find you guilty of treason if you don't hate Putin; The whole thing is simply a "border dispute"; "Ukraine is not a democracy"; Ukraine is a "puppet" of the West; and ...unless Vladimir Putin has personally had you or one of your family members murdered, you really don't have any right to criticize the guy." *Tucker Carlson Hoping We Can Just Forget About All the Times He Insisted Putin Was the Best,* Bess Levin, Vanity Fair, February 25, 2022.

231   *A Free and Responsible Press.* Five functions of a socially responsible press, based on the 1947 Hutchins Commission report: 1. The press should offer a truthful, comprehensive account of the day's events in a context which gives them meaning. Perspective is important, not only objectivity. 2. The press should serve as a forum for comment and criticism. 3. The press should offer a representative picture of constituent groups in society; that is, no stereotyping. 4. The press should transmit cultural heritage, present and clarify goals and values for society. 5. The press should offer full access to the day's intelligence, that is, to reflect the public's right to know.

232   On March 25, 2022, President Joe Biden recalled that Xi Jinping, President of China, mentioned this in a recent conversation.

233   For the full text go to: https://www.britannica.com/event/Gettysburg-Address

234  *Team of Rivals*, Pages 484-86 and 52-25.

235  "The Revolutionary War brought another opportunity for people of all races to participate in state-sanctioned armed combat. Thousands of enslaved Blacks chose to join British forces, serving the Crown in exchange for their freedom. On the American side, free blacks in New England, already members of the militia before the war started, decided to fight for the ideals of the patriots, and were on many early battlefields, including Bunker Hill, Concord and Saratoga." *American Revolution is a multiracial story*, Susan Nevins, Rutland Herald, August 22, 2020.

236  "During the American Revolution, the majority of American Indian Nations allied themselves with the British in order to preserve their culture and stop encroachment upon their lands. However, some supported the Patriots and their cause because of personal ties, shared religious beliefs, or mistreatment by the British in the past. These allies included large numbers from the Oneidas, Tuscaroras, Mohicans, and the Stockbridge-Munsee Nations." *American Indian Allies at Valley Forge*, Valley Forge National Historical Park Website.

237  *The Cultural Origins of Human Cognition*, Page 193.

238  "Concerts, dance recitals and exhibitions have been postponed indefinitely after Vladimir Putin's invasion of Ukraine." *The show can't go on: Russian arts cancelled worldwide*, Nadia Khomami, The Guardian, March 1, 2022.

239  "With Malice Toward None..." Lincoln's Second Inaugural Address, National Park Service Website.

240  At the end of the Civil War, Lincoln insisted on lenient terms for Lee and his officers, allowing them to return to their homes rather than imprisoning them,

which was to their surprise. *Team of Rivals*, Page 725.

241  "He treated me like a man; he did not let me feel for a moment that there was any difference in the color of our skins!" *Team of Rivals*, Page 650.